THE SON OF MAN

The German original of this work, published by Ernst Rowohlt Verlag, Berlin,
1928, is entitled DER MENSCHENSOHN,
GESCHICHTE EINES PROPHETEN.

EMIL LUDWIG

has also written

NAPOLEON

BISMARCK

WILHELM II

THE SON OF MAN

by

E M I L   L U D W I G

Translated
From the German by
Eden & Cedar
Paul

With eight illustrations after
Rembrandt

LONDON
ERNEST BENN LIMITED

First published in
May, 1928.
Second impression
May, 1928.

Printed
in
Great Britain

IN MEMORIAM
HUJUS AETATIS
MARTYRUM

PUBLISHER'S NOTE

The wording of some of the quotations in THE
SON OF MAN differs from the familiar text of
the authorised version of the New Testament.
Herr Ludwig has not only combined passages
from the various Gospels, but has modernised
the phrasing. In accordance with his express
wishes, the translators have followed the same
plan in preparing the English version.

CONTENTS

ILLUSTRATIONS

TO THE READER

THE world is familiar with the general substance of that part of the history of my race which is retold in the ensuing chapters. Furthermore, the attempt to write the life of Jesus from a purely historical standpoint, is older than the days of the Enlightenment.

Could biographical portraiture be more difficult than in the present instance? We have to depict a man concerning whom practically nothing is known until he reached the age of thirty, least of all his personal appearance, the mirror of the soul ; whilst of the two years, more or less, which preceded his early death, we have only conflicting stories. The gospels, the four main sources of knowledge, contradict one another in many respects, and are upon some points contradicted by the scanty non-Christian authorities. Thus even the material we have must be carefully sifted.

Moreover, there is a confusion in the serial arrangement, a confusion which has been deplored throughout the centuries. We have accounts of very little more than the beginning

and the end, the baptism and the trial. What
lies between is chaotic. "The gospels," wrote
Luther, " do not keep order in their account of
the miracles and deeds of Jesus. This is of small
moment. When there is a dispute about Holy
Writ, and no comparison is possible, let the matter
drop." Almost all the contradictions arise out
of the disorderly nature of the reports. As soon
as we arrange them psychologically, everything
is seen to be logical. Not till then do the two
great periods in Jesus' life become comprehen-
sible : the period of humble-minded but cheerful
teaching ; and the period when he was filled
with the consciousness of a Messianic mission.
When the account of the latter period is made to
follow the account of the former in a natural
fashion, the character of Jesus is freed from its
contradictions, and manifests a human, a simple,
course of development.

This book deals with " Jesus," and has not a
word to say about " Christ." The author does
not meddle with theology ; that arose later, and
he does not pretend to understand it. He tells
the story as if the tremendous consequences of the
life he describes were unknown to him—as they
were unknown to Jesus, and unwilled. The
book, therefore, ignores the interpolations in the
gospels, whether made retrospectively to show

the confirmation of ancient prophecies, or pro-
spectively to provide support for the still youthful Church. Much has been omitted because
modern research has rejected it as spurious.
If the reader misses some text endeared to him
from childhood, let him remember that libraries
are filled with discussions as to the genuineness
of such passages. Since in these days most
persons derive their impressions of the story of
Jesus from pictures of a comparatively recent
date rather than from the gospels, a good deal
escapes their notice. They fail, for instance, to
observe that neither in Mark nor in Matthew
are we told that Jesus visited the temple when he
was a child, and that only one of the four evan-
gelists says that Mary and John were present
when he died on the cross.

In this account, when any reference is made
to the miracles, they are interpreted natural-
istically, for I am writing history and building
up a picture of human characters. All Jesus'
miracles might be shown to have been no
miracles, or a hundred new miracles might be
successfully ascribed to him ; neither the one nor
the other would diminish his greatness. That
is why I have made so little use of the gospel of
John, which has been most exposed to the fire
of modern criticism, and have drawn mainly

upon the accounts of Mark and Matthew. But I have combined all the reports in such a way as will best elucidate the incident with which I am dealing.

On the other hand, nothing has been super-added ; that is why the book is short. The mishmash which is called a historical novel caricaturing, as Goethe said, both romance and history, and hardly practicable when the sources are so exiguous, would have been in this case immoral as well. One who would venture to ascribe to Jesus imaginary sayings and doings, should be a person at least equal to Jesus in intuitive power. Chapter and verse in one or more of the gospels can be given for everything that Jesus is here portrayed as having said or done ; only in outlooks and methods of ex-pression, only in the bridges of thought whereby the words and the deeds are interconnected, has the author necessarily given free rein to imagina-tion. Since I have endeavoured to do this in a purely human way, by telling of human con-flicts and inhibitions and resolves, I may hope that my account will not arouse that sense of something utterly remote from contemporary experience which continually disturbs the modern reader of the gospels, and drags him out of the depths into the shallows. If the attempt to give a coloured picture (an attempt which misleads us into an excessive use of imagination) were to be avoided, nothing remained but to limn this portrait after the manner of a woodcut.

Far from its being my purpose to shake the faith which those who live in Christ have in the divinity of Christ, my aim, rather, is to convince those who regard the personality of Jesus as artificially constructed, that he is a real and intensely human figure. "Had he never lived," says Rousseau, "the writers of the gospels would themselves have been as great as Jesus."

My aim is, not to expound teaching with which all are familiar, but to portray the inner life of the prophet. What interests us here is, not his later influence, exercised through the instrumentality of others, but the world of his own feelings. The development of that world of self-feeling, the aims and motives of a leader, his struggles and weaknesses and disappointments ; the great spiritual battle between self-assertion and humility, between responsibility and discouragement, between the claims of his mission and his longing for personal happiness— these must be described. A prophet was to be portrayed, a man greater than all his contemporaries and nevertheless unable to cope with the world into which he had been born. Not that the author supposes the interpretation here put forward to be the only one conceivable ! It is one among many possible interpretations, and aspires, at least, to be in harmony with the spirit of our own time.

In a prelude, I give the political and mental atmosphere out of which a prophet of such a kind and of such a way of thinking could emerge. The manner in which he welded together, remodelled, and made glorious the catchwords of his day, would alone suffice to prove the greatness of his genius.

Yet the key to his nature is found, not in his genius, but in his human heart.

Moscia, 1927.

PRELUDE

JERUSALEM

I.

NIGHT still broods in the halls of the temple. The priests who are keeping watch peer through the darkness. Some of them are crouching, others lying. They can see one another only in dim outlines, can just discern the shadowy movements of one another's arms as they draw their mantles more closely round them ; they can recognise one another only by the murmur of voices. Through the arcades of the upper terrace, the wind from the sea blows keen, for the end of March is near, and the waters are vexed by the equinoctial gales. At the foot of the Holy of Holies the great stone city lies slumbering. All are asleep : Jews and Gentiles ; sages, beggars, and rich men ; priests and people ; pride and wisdom. There is much hatred betwixt house and house ; but in the houses, love. Little joy but much hope—for it is a conquered city, and the conquered despise their conquerors. Power lies asleep in Jerusalem ; the cold steel weapons do not stir, nor

2

do harsh commands break the silence of the
night. Peace seems to breathe down from the
firmament, now that for a generation and more
there has been no clash of arms in the Jewish
capital. Nevertheless, hatred of the conquerors
smoulders in the hearts of the people. Even
while the conquered are sleeping and while hate
is in abeyance in their relaxed limbs, still through
the dreams of men and women alike looms faith
in the one God. " He will return as King of
the Jews and Lord of the world !"

Now comes a sound of heavy footsteps, the
measured tread of armed men. Light flickers
through the arches of the hall, vanishes for a
moment, and then returns in force. Those who
are lying on the ground leap to their feet. It
is the captain of the temple who has come with
his men. Thrice every night this guard makes
the round. The pretext is that the Romans are
watching over the safety of the holy hill, but in
truth they have an eye to their own safety as
well. In the flicker of the torches, the two parties
glare at one another while their traditional
enmity gleams in their eyes. No one speaks.
Enough that they see one another, while orders
are fulfilled.

What do the priests see in the torchlight?
They see men who are sturdy rather than tall ;
men whose harness in this illumination has a
golden-red sheen ; men whose arms and legs are

bare, while their bodies are clad in scale-armour. Some of them carry spears ; others, swords. The faces beneath the hemispherical helmets are beardless, brown, and wiry ; faces showing hardness and reserve ; the faces of young men who think little, but can make long marches. Men who laugh readily, eat heartily, and are prone to be rough-and-ready wooers. The captain, whose armour is half hidden by a cloak, has gentler lineaments, and seems lost in thought. In truth, it is his way to hide the scorn with which the sight of these priests inspires him. For his part, as he contemplates the Israelites, he sees bent figures, some long and lean, some short and stout, all wearing gaberdines which fall from their shoulders to their sandals ; men with yellow faces, black hair, and black beards. Men who are wearied with watching, and who fear their Roman conquerors. Yet from their dark eyes flash fanaticism, hope, and pride.

Thus do the two worlds face one another, men of faith and men of war, conquered and conquerors. Thus do the Jews and the Romans face one another this night in Jerusalem.

Three hours later, the sun has risen behind the bare hills eastward of Jordan, revealing the familiar scene to the priests and the soldiers who comprise this twofold temple guard. Rocky hills, grey and yellow, cold and repellent, water- less and well-nigh treeless, surround the great

white town wherein rocks and walls seem one.
The place was a natural fortress, and all that
human hands need do was to crown the rocky
rampart with walls, combining the whole with
simple art, until the city was fitted into its place
among the five hills.

Where they are standing, upon the flattened
summit which Solomon long since had levelled
for the first temple, the second temple, begun
after the return from Babylon, now rises. Looking south-westward, their eyes rest on another
hill, on which clear-cut shadows are cast by the
rising sun. To this a bridge leads. Taller and
finer than the temple hill is the Mount of Zion,
where in the days beyond recall (days for whose
return devout Jews hope unceasingly) King
David had built his stronghold. On Zion are
the homes of the well-to-do. Northward, facing
this eminence, is the detested acropolis of the
Romans, Antonia by name, on the hilltop which
the Maccabees had fortified two hundred years
earlier, when Israel rose against the heathen.
Behind, on the marshy ground to the north of
the town, dwell the poorer folk. Thus he who
holds the fortress commands the temple and the
gates, controls the metropolis of this turbulent
nation, sits astride the southern end of the
narrow land—which, it seems, might be crossed
in a few strides from the desert to the
Mediterranean shore.

II.

Below, in the crowded dwellings, the people
are now awake. There is stir and bustle and
colour in the narrow streets. The cries of the
street sellers are echoing from the stone walls.
Many thousand strangers throng the town.
Three days from now comes the Feast of Passover ;
the inns and their stables are filled with men
and camels. Workers and traders, shoemakers
and tailors, barbers and scribes, vendors of
vegetables and dried figs, are plying for custom.
Asses, heavily laden, are driven from street to
street, carrying merchandise to prospective
buyers.

The general movement is towards the temple
hill, although there is nothing more afoot there
than on any other day. Built in a square, five
hundred ells each side, its walls are surmounted
by three great terraces. Towards these the
crowd is moving, to gain the huge lower arcades,
where no business is done, but where we meet
every one. This is the outer court, the court
of the heathen, placarded with inscriptions in
Greek and Latin warning unbelievers against
access to the second terrace. Nineteen steps
separate the faithful from the unfaithful, and
every Gentile knows that to mount these steps
is for him a crime punishable with death.

On the lower terrace, then, Romans and Greeks must stay their steps, though the former belong to the conquering race, and the latter may be rich merchants. Here, too, Arabs and Babylonians, anciently at war one with another, and aforetime masters of this city, must likewise pause. Farther than this no unbeliever may go. Proud, therefore, are the Jews that even the poorest and raggedest among them may climb the nineteen great steps to the second terrace, to stand in the inner court between high walls, amid tall columns, gazing yet higher, up the twelve steps that lead to the innermost temple on the crown of the hilltop, where, as all know, is the Holy of Holies.

The crowd is waiting. Up there the priests have left their cells, have performed their ablutions, have put on clean raiment. Now they are preparing for their daily duties. One must slay the morning sacrifice ; another must lay the firing upon the altar ; another must clear away the ashes, must see to the incense, must trim the lights, must replenish the shew-bread, must care for the vessels. All is made ready. The lamb is led to the altar, beside which in the twilight each takes up his position. Are the singers in their places ? Are the basins ready ? Some one gives a signal. Slowly, with a harsh clangour, the huge gates yield to the pressure of many hands, and open. A trumpet sounds

thrice, and, from the two terraces below, all
eyes are uplifted. At this instant, the morning
sacrifice is slain; its blood consecrates the
temple. Then the priests move in procession
into the pillared halls. Prayers follow, and the
commandments are read. When the incense
is burned on the golden altar, the priests, too,
prostrate themselves, the Levites clash metal
basins together, there is playing of zithers and
harps, the chorus intones a psalm, whose eight
intervals are punctuated with trumpet-blasts, and
at each blast the members of the congregation
prostrate themselves anew.

As the day advances, the courts of the temple
become ever more crowded. At noon, when
the second service is at hand, there is a babel of
voices, for the market is in full swing. Down
below, in the court of the heathen, everything
is bought and sold—everything which Jews can
sell and foreigners can buy. The livelong day,
an old man sitting on the steps offers a he-goat
for sale. Should he get a good price for the
beast, he will have enough to live upon for three
months to come. If only one of the wealthy
Jews from Alexandria, visiting Jerusalem for the
Passover, would realise what a fine beast this
goat is, and how pleasing to God would be such
a sacrifice. Flocks and herds are driven in.
Buying, selling, and barter go on from hour to
hour. There is incense of all colours and

perfumes. There is amber from Asia and frank-
incense from Egypt. Twigs of palm can be
bought as mementoes. Scrolls can be purchased, notable texts from the prophets, inscribed
upon parchment in the strong and virile Hebrew
characters, or in the more elegant and feminine
script of the Greeks. The various traders are
chattering and shouting, bargaining and cheat-
ing. Squatting behind small tables are the
money-changers, whose privileged places are
handed down from father to son. The money-
changers are an essential part of the pageant,
for Greek and Roman coins, bearing a human
effigy, are not accepted within the temple.
Jews from foreign parts must change the money
they have brought with them before they can
pay the temple dues, or give alms to the poor.

Mendicant pilgrims stand on the steps, quiet
amid the din. In Athens or Syracuse, in
Morocco or Gaul, for years past they have looked
forward to this day when they would be able to
gaze upon the great home of their faith, the second
temple which had taken the place of the first,
the temple richly endowed by Herod. Now,
praying as they go, they slowly, and with ecstasy,
make their way upwards to the holy gates.
There it is, the multi-coloured, embroidered
curtain of which their fathers have told them ;
and there, too, is the golden vine, emblem of
fertility ! At last they will be able to enter the

vestibule, and to place amid the thousands of costly thankofferings, the ones they themselves have brought with them, the fruit of painful savings, the thankofferings they clutched to their bosoms when storm-tossed on the seas, the thankofferings they hid beneath their pillows when sleeping overnight in the inn. Looking towards the dim recesses of the Holy of Holies, they picture in imagination what they hope to see on the day of festival—the brazen basin upborne by oxen, symbol of the waters upon which, in the beginning, the spirit of God moved.

Seated round a pillar are half a dozen or so young men regardless of the clamour made by the praying strangers and the chattering traders. They are listening to a learned rabbi who reads from the ancient texts and expounds them. Every one is free to interrupt the teacher, for the best scholar is he who is most eager to question, and even children are entitled to reasonable answers. Soon the lesson becomes a dialogue, and one who makes his mark in this combat of ideas, one who with keen analysis is able to disclose some unexpected though valuable interpretation of the law, comes quickly to the front, and will himself ere long be noted as a learned expositor.

At length the teacher cuts these ambitious disciples short, for below he sees a long train of peasants from Galilee, newly arrived. He knows

them by their dress. They have spent the night
in the open ; now they are leading in the ox
they have brought for the sacrifice, an ox with
gilded horns ; and they bring with them in
baskets the first-fruits of their fields. The priests
go down to meet them, and the procession sings :
" Our feet stand within thy gates, O Jerusalem."
Behind them comes a second caravan, composed
of pilgrims from afar, richly clad men riding
on camels. These bring, as offerings, treasures
wrapped in linen cloths.

III.

Through the broiling sunshine of noon, the
priests make their way to the fortress of the
Roman governor. Down one hill and up another—so close are Rome and Judea ! But the
common folk who line the streets through which
the procession passes, recognise that there is an
invisible chasm between the two hills, and they
murmur at the slavery betokened by this visit
which is the prelude to every festival. It must be
in order to humiliate the chosen people that four
times every year the governor comes to the fortress
of Antonia, to give the thousands who flock to
Jerusalem from afar a plain demonstration of the
fact that Rome rules. He keeps the sacred
raiment under lock and key, handing it over
on each occasion to those who ask for it—as a

loan merely. Why should the high priest's
mantle be kept in the hands of the heathen from
festival to festival? To cleanse it from heathen
contamination, long exposure to the fumes of
incense is needed!

Now the priests enter the gate of the fortress.
The governor stands to receive them.

As officer in command of the legion, he
wears helmet and chain, and his sword clanks
as he salutes the priests. They make profound
obeisance, and await his pleasure. Two soldiers
bring the coffer, which is doubly sealed. The
governor breaks the Roman seals; and then the
priests break their own seals which, after long
argument, they too have been privileged to
affix. From the coffer they take the robes,
heavy with gold and precious stones. Without
a word, farewell salutes are exchanged. The
Jews depart, carrying the robes back to the
temple.

Pilate's heart is hot within him. The pride
of these Jews is the pride which apes humility!
Rome has subjugated half the world. Will she
never be able to conquer this small and weakly
people? Five years and more he has ruled
here in the name of the emperor, and although
in his reports he speaks of tranquillity and
obedience, he knows that beneath the surface
a spirit of revolt is seething, ready at any moment
to burst forth. How preposterous it is that he

cannot have the emperor's image stamped
on the Jewish coins. What harm would the
portrait of the emperor do to these lunatics?
Though the emperor be honoured as a god, he
is but emperor ; where else in the world was a
people whose god was king? What did they
mean by their City of God? No one interfered
with their customs in the temple ; Rome had
never forced her own gods upon the barbarians.
Why, then, should there be this perpetual uproar
about a few images, a few ideas?

When he had first taken up his post, he had
sent, over night, the banners with the emperor's
silver shield to the Jerusalem garrison. Thereupon a riot had broken out. The Jews had
flocked in thousands to Cæsarea. For five days
and five nights they had camped outside the
fortress. He had surrounded them with his
soldiers, and had threatened to cut them all
down if they did not go home. Thereupon they
bared their necks for the stroke ; they would
rather die ! What could he do? He had had
to fetch back the eagles and the shield from the
Holy City.

What they really cared about was the fees
paid to the temple ! Though they were always
grumbling at the moderate Roman taxes, they
paid the temple dues willingly enough. The
only object of such revolts was to prevent Rome
from controlling their money ! What tricks

might they not play with all the money brought
by the pilgrims flocking to that hill over there?
If there were any further disturbances in Jerusalem, if there was more rioting in Galilee, if the
Romans should be worsted in some street affray,
when the news of these matters reached Rome it
would go hard with the governor.

Pilate's thoughts turned to Rome. He wondered whether his powerful patron, Sejanus,
was still alive. Who could tell? Perhaps the
emperor was dead! Pilate's wife had visions;
made him anxious when she told him her dreams.
—The governor muses. He thinks of the
emperor.

Tiberius, a lonely old man, dwelt at Capri.
The lord of the world, the Roman emperor,
had for years now been living in this little isle,
far from the capital, neglecting the affairs of
government, gloomy, morose, inactive. High
up among the rocks, he had built himself
a stronghold whence he looked down across
the sea, passing the weary hours in mystical
calculations. One day his mood would be
indifferent, another day it would be cruel; one
day he would pardon, another day he would kill;
one day he would restrict the freedoms of the
people, another day he would enlarge them. A
sombre dictator was Tiberius, entrusting his
powers to the hands of others, withdrawing these
powers without notice—suspicious, dour, melan-

choly. Had he profited from the outpourings
of blood for which he had been responsible?
He had lost his only son, but had been unable
to take vengeance. Feelings of hatred were
universal. The prætorians distrusted Sejanus;
the emperor distrusted the prætorians; everyone
distrusted the emperor. Only on this island of
Capri could he be safe! Where else could the
lord of the world seek refuge?

In philosophy perchance?

Seneca, in his last epistle, had written of
Diogenes: " It is worth a kingdom, to be, in a
world of cheats, murderers, and kidnappers,
the only person whom no one can injure!"
The emperor sends for Seneca's new discourse
and reads: " We have all erred, and on into our
old age we shall continue to fail in our duty.
The evil does not lie outside us; it is intertwined
with our own entrails. The body is nothing
but the burden and punishment of the spirit.
The soul strives to return to the place whence it
came. There waits eternal calm, and there, after
the confusions of the world, lucidity prevails.
The day is coming which will free you from the
tabernacle of this hateful life. To be fettered,
mutilated, crucified—these are the signs of
virtue."

That sounds akin to the strange faith of
Jerusalem! The emperor's thoughts turn to the
Jews, to whom in Rome he has entrusted so

much business on his own behalf and on that of
the State. He had sent munificent gifts to their
temple, and had a bull and two lambs sacrificed
there daily, in honour of the Most High God.
Who is the Most High God? Just as little as
Seneca, could the Jews limn his portrait or name
his holy name. But did their god save them
when he, their emperor, had suddenly withdrawn
his favour from the tribe he had hitherto protected? No, their god had not extended a
helping hand ; but thousands of them had let
themselves be sent to the penal legion rather
than burn their sacred utensils. Strange people,
these Jews ! He had had his own son Drusus
educated in the company of young Herod ; the
two lads had been fond of one another. When
Drusus was murdered, Herod had been sent
away from the court, for his presence was a
painful reminder to the emperor. Now the
emperor had sent for Herod, had summoned him
to Capri as the last witness of that crime.
Tiberius wanted to see the young sprig of Jewish
royalty once more, before following his own son.
Following whither? Seneca said that death
was peace.

As he turned these things over in his mind,
Pilate's thoughts flitted to and fro between
Capri and Rome. If he had but been able to
enrich himself like Varus ! Pilate was no worse
than another governor—though cruel at times,

arrogant, and ill-tempered, as was natural to a
man in the dull seclusion of colonial life. Like
his predecessors, he had farmed out the customs
dues and the taxes. What did it matter to him
that the country groaned under the exactions of
the tax-gatherers and the usurers, who extracted
far more from the people than was handed
over to the governor? The tax-gatherers were
rascals to whose word no one gave credence
in the courts. Pilate's own hands were clean.

IV.

That afternoon, in one of the cool, stone-
walled rooms of the temple, between the
sanctuary and the outer court, the supreme
council of the Jews was sitting. This council,
the Sanhedrim, was composed of the most noted
priests, men well on in years, some of them
white-haired. In the place of honour sat Joseph
Caiphas, the high priest, the leader of the
nation. Caiphas was high priest before Pilate
came to Judea as governor. Pilate had merely
confirmed him in his post. The decisions of the
Sanhedrim required nothing more than the
formal approval of the governor. It functioned
as a supreme court both temporal and spiritual,
as simultaneously court of justice and senate.
Its decisions were irrevocable. All the Jews,
both at home and abroad, even princes and high

priests, were subject to its decrees. Only when it enacted the death penalty, decided by an open vote, was the approval of the Roman governor necessary before the sentence could be carried out. This supreme council was a self-appointed body, a preserve of the old rabbinical families. As a hereditary chamber of elderly men, it was extremely conservative, so that the Romans tried to secure the election of wealthy persons of tolerant views.

Such were the Sadducees, a small though influential body of patricians, who were loath to let their pleasures, their privileges, and the power of the dominant class, be endangered by a defiant attitude towards the conquerors or by any undue display of religious zeal. The law of Moses, said the Sadducees, stands as of old, and we will keep it ; but the commentaries of later days, added since that law was first revealed, are not the word of the prophet, and are no concern of ours. Where is it written that we may not lay up treasure to ourselves, that we must not eat from silver platters, that we are not entitled to enjoy the pleasures that God has given us ? True that the Romans are unclean ; but so long as we keep the feast days in due order, we are not forbidden to share in the good things the Romans bring us.

The people cannot understand such sophistications, nor should it do so. Offer the common

folk anything other than temporal rewards:
a long life, as promised by the prophets, lived
righteously, without either fears or hopes concerning an existence beyond the grave. Show
them that they will live on in the persons of their
children, and let them seek the blessings of the
man whose quiver is full.

Cheek by jowl with such opulent and easy-
going fellows (easy-going in doctrinal matters,
though strict enough in their judgment of the
things of this world), sit in the Sanhedrim their
enemies, lean elders, sour-faced, eyes aglow with
fanaticism. These are the Pharisees, the name
meaning " the pure " or " those set apart."
They are members of the great nationalist party,
born democrats, and democrats both in theory
and practice. There are six thousand of them,
well versed in the latest commentaries. These
priests are, almost all of them, sons and brothers
of blacksmiths, curriers, coopers, woodmen,
sandal-makers, and the like. It is a rule of
party discipline that they shall do manual work
for at least one-third of every day ; or else that
they shall do manual work in summer while
devoting the winter to their studies. Most of
them are poor, and it is a matter of strict prin-
ciple with them never to take money or money's
worth for expounding the scriptures. Therefore
they are honoured by the people.

Nevertheless, with puritanical zeal, they hold

aloof from the everyday life of the common
folk from whom they spring. While renouncing
the pursuit of power, pleasure, and pelf (to
which their foes, the aristocratic Sadducees,
are addicted), they plume themselves upon
their intimate knowledge of Holy Writ, upon
their skill as expounders and controversialists.
Swollen with spiritual pride, they despise their
own brethren—peasants, craftsmen, and journey-
men—who cannot read the scriptures, do not
sedulously observe the law, are not able to understand the commentaries. The phylacteries
which are conspicuous on their arms, and the
large fringes with which their garments are
bordered, are to keep them ever mindful of the
law.

The way in which they reckon up the effect
which every sacrifice may have in attracting
God's favour, their parade of long prayers and of
flagellations and of almsgiving, their excess of
zeal in the matter of fasts and purifications, their
self-righteous airs in face of those who are less
strict than themselves in point of ritual observance, their insistence that no hour must ever
be forgotten and no rule ever disregarded, their
sedulousness to heed the prohibitions even more
faithfully than the positive commandments—
these characteristics make them leaders in the
education of the people, and also the butt of
sceptically minded individuals, so that their

adversaries the Sadducees sometimes ask quiz-
zically, when the Pharisees intend to begin
cleaning up the sun.

With them, works count, not faith. One who
offers up many sacrifices in the temple is quit
of the duty of maintaining his aged parents.
In their educational discourses they speak, not
of sin or conscience or adultery, but of how many
paces it is permissible to walk on the Sabbath
day. Could they get their way, the number
of strokes with the rod in a penal flogging would
be reduced from forty to thirty-nine. For years
they have eagerly discussed the question whether
the corn for the sacrifice on the second day of the
Passover may lawfully be cut on the Sabbath.
Is it binding to swear by the temple, or only
by the gold of the temple? Is a woman in
childbed unclean for one week only, or for two?
On days of atonement, when incense is burned
before the Holy of Holies, should it be kindled
before or after the entrance of the high priest?

While with their dogmas and their textual
criticism the Pharisees were thus tending to
choke morality with tares, these same men were
sending forth to the people a message of hope.
There would come a new Moses, a new liberator.
Never must the Jews forget that they were the
chosen people. Theirs was the City of God,
and it was their part to despise the heathen.
Just as their fathers had refused to swear fealty

to the false house of Herod, so now must they
renounce allegiance to the Romans.

What is the business before the Sanhedrim
to-day? The councillors are discussing, which
among certain condemned criminals shall be
set free by the Romans. For a generation, now,
the Jews have been privileged, on the day of
Passover, to demand from the governor grace
for an offender. Whose life shall they ask Pilate
to spare?

V.

At this hour, when the shadows are lengthening,
the well-to-do among the pilgrims are being
borne through the streets in litters. Though
from time to time they close the curtains, as if
embarrassed by the gaze of the crowd, in truth
it tickles their vanity to be stared at.

They do not attract so much attention in the
great cities from which they come! Compared
with Rome or Alexandria, the once mighty
Jerusalem has shrunk to the dimensions of a
mere country town, the capital of one poor
province. Overseas, in the metropolis of the
empire, they breathe the air of two-and-twenty
provinces, among which obscure and tiny Palestine is almost a nonentity. A poor little country
—what are its exports? Some oil, some fruit,
no more. No more, except for the keen, clear
spirit which from this out-of-the-way corner

spreads far and wide through the world; the proud and stubborn faith in the one God, of whom no graven images may be fashioned; the stiff-necked resolve which made the children of Israel refuse to honour the kings of the earth, and even the emperor, by prostrating themselves before a sculptured semblance; the Jews' persistent and loudly proclaimed hope that Jehovah would one day cast down the old gods from their seats. Tidings of these strange, bold tenets have carried the name of Israel into all the centres of culture and worship, arousing there a modicum of consternation. A weak people and a small, yet one whose name has resounded mightily in the world of wealth and power. Some, indeed, are prone to mock at the Jews; others are secretly afraid of them, dreading the incorruptibility of their doctrine, and thinking it better to leave them severely alone.

The men who, robed in silk, are now being carried through the narrow alleys by their slaves, are themselves the grandchildren of slaves. Pompey, the triumvir, the first Roman conqueror of Jerusalem, had brought back a number of Jews in bondage to grace his triumph, and had freed most of them ere long. Huddled together, to begin with, on the island in the Tiber, they had made their living as small traders. When Julius Cæsar rose to power, recognising the abilities of these freedmen from Palestine, he

had encouraged them by his patronage, had
given them the franchise, and had turned their
commercial abilities to account by using them as
intermediaries for the supply of grain and
munitions of war. In a word, they inspired so
much confidence that they soon became bankers
to the emperor, the creditors of dethroned kings,
lessees of theatres and ballets, even while some
of them were performers on the boards. Versa-
tile, supple, endowed with a talent for languages,
they were equipped with all the merits and all
the defects of the Levantines.

This colony of Jews in Rome, eight thousand
strong (for the numbers were soon swelled by
migrants and adventurers), though it so quickly
gained wealth and influence, preserved its isolation in the great city. Very few lapsed into
paganism. True, many of them took Latin
names and adopted Roman manners ; many of
them frequented the barbarian games ; many of
them ceased to boast of being circumcised. Yet
most of them continued to profess the old faith
openly enough. Except for business purposes,
they would not mix with the heathen. Con-
versely, it became the fashion for the pagans to
Judaise a little. The Roman ladies, in especial,
bored to death and seeking for a new sensation,
flocked to the synagogues. Afterwards, reclining
at dinner—when they were toying with roast
peacock from Samos or lampreys from Tartessus

or mussels from Chios, or when (after taking a
vomit and while awaiting the revival of appetite)
they were watching the change of table-furniture
and hangings that was to give the illusion of a
new banqueting hall—these luxurious dames
would find the moment apt for lively converse
about the one and invisible God.

Had not the old gods long since been a-dying?
The Stoics made no secret of their views, dis-
claiming polytheism, and quoting Plato, who,
three centuries before the time of Julius Cæsar,
had lamented that the soul should fall out of the
ethereal world to be prisoned in the body, and
had looked forward joyfully to the day when it
would return to its own element.   Was that a
reason, however, for renouncing the joys of the
flesh?   In answer, read Seneca!   At once philosopher and man of the world, at once priest of
the soul and political orator, this sage had written
not long ago : " A life without perturbation and
without misadventure is like a dead sea.   God our
Father has put ready to our hand all good things
to serve our purposes.   Not tarrying for our
prayers, he gave us these things out of his own
bounty."

" God our Father."   What a magnificent idea!
But then, if we all had one father, all human
beings would be equal by birth.   Terrible
thought!   Yet Seneca goes even further, writing :
" Slaves are something more than fellow-men,

housemates, and friends ; they are fellow-slaves !
The goods that accrue to us—children, honours,
a woman's charms—are not out-and-out property.
They are but things lent, to soften the asperities
of our earthly pilgrimage. Just as the furnish-
ings of an inn belong to the innkeeper, and not
to the traveller who has the use of them, so do
these our ' belongings ' return to the Lord of
all when our earthly course is run." If our
slaves hear this message (think the fine folk), the
pillars of world empire will be shaken !

Still, in the end, Seneca's gospel is none so
bad.—" Be swift to take delight in your children.
Pluck the fruit of pleasure while ye may. Love
what brings joy as something of which you must
make the most in life's fleeting hour."—Well,
Epicurus said much the same, though the Greek
sage would perhaps have warned us against
eating so many oysters and truffles !

Such are the musings of the powerful in Rome,
as they try to dispel their growing uneasiness by
antidotal wafts of alien doctrine. For the times
are out of joint. Very rich there are, and very
poor ; the middle class has almost disappeared.
Out-of-works abound ; they throng the streets,
a myriad idlers, fed on doles from the State
granaries. A rabble of adventurers, informers,
secret poisoners, and spies thrive in a society
whose foundations they are sapping, what time,
under the empire, the thrifty life of old republican

days has passed away for ever. The prefects
are intriguing against the prætorians, the prætorians against the favourites, and the favourites
against the absentee emperor. Meanwhile, the
luxury of the ruling class seems like a rock against
which the waves of poverty foam in vain ; but
new waves are roaring behind ; the earth quakes
beneath the huge palaces ; the lords of this
world are prudent, and would fain, if they could,
find reinsurance in a life beyond the grave.
Who can tell whether this ancient god of the
Jews or the new gods of whom other sophists
talk, may not be all the more powerful because
they are invisible ?

The wealthy Roman Jew, now being carried
through the streets of the Holy City in his litter,
follows in imagination these thoughts of his
pagan acquaintances in the city of the Seven
Hills. Arrived at the inn where he will take up
his quarters during the festival, he may chance
to encounter a business friend from Alexandria,
and the two merchants will exchange news. The
Alexandrian will tell the tale of the bankruptcy
of a discrowned king, coupling his story with
an account of the deeds and the sayings of the
Jewish community in Egypt, and of how far the
Jewish spirit and faith have been kept peculiar
or have been tinctured with Greek culture.
The Jew of Rome will indeed hear wonderful
tidings from the Jew of Alexandria.

For the Jews have been back in Egypt ('tis
but two or three days' voyage from coast to
coast) since the beginning of the Ptolemaic era.
Now there are one million persons of Hebrew
descent in the land of the lower Nile. In
Alexandria, the children of Israel comprise not
less than half of all the free population ; two
districts of the city are wholly under their con-
trol ; they almost monopolise the trade between
East and West ; all the great shipping lines have
been in their hands since Emperor Augustus
entrusted them with the supervision of the Nile
and the Delta—a signal mark of confidence,
seeing that Egypt is the granary of Rome.

Nay more, Alexandria had been the intel-
lectual metropolis of the world two centuries and
more before Rome had become the political
capital. Was it to be expected that, in this
city, the Jews would withstand the influences
of Greek art, whose treasures had since the
days of Alexander been making their way in
ever-increasing numbers southward across the
Mediterranean? Not, of course, that the temple
of Alexandria was to be contaminated by traces
of heathen art ! The temple, in its splendour
and its purity, was to vie with the mother-temple
in Jerusalem. Furthermore, if the Egyptian
Jews read the works of Homer and Plato, these
were romances, which could not affect the solid
world of theocratic fact. In the days of the first

Ptolemies the books of Moses and the books of
Solomon, all the laws and all the wisdom of
the Jews, had been rendered into Greek, and
thus the secrets of the chosen people had been
made known to the whole world. When the
seventy-two elders, six from each tribe, secluded
on an island, had in seventy-two days (thus ran
the legend) completed the Septuagint version
of the Pentateuch, this momentous undertaking
cut them off from their narrow tribalism to
become citizens of the world. These ancient
worthies praised the day when they handed the
golden book, penned in Greek, to the learned
king, Ptolemy Philadelphus, who had com-
missioned them to make the translation for his
library. Now the world would learn that Moses
had been a greater man than Pythagoras.

The Jew from Rome has a matter of more
topical interest, about which he wishes to
question the Jew from Alexandria. What news
of Philo ? Is he to go on a new mission to the
emperor ? What about his latest book, the one
concerning dreams ; is it of a very startling
character ? How soon will a transcript be
obtainable ? Does Philo go too far, after all,
so that his writings tend to shake people's faith
in the words of the prophets ?

Philo the Jew, shining star of Greek Judaism,
is at this time a man nearing sixty. A child
of both the worlds that touch beside the waters

of the lower Nile, he combines in his writings the streams of thought that are confluent in the delta of the epoch in which he lives. He is a citizen of the first world-wide empire, a disciple of two cultures, a sage whose lot is cast in the great seaport to which the sailing ships and the galleys bring goods and ideas. Open-minded, almost entirely free from national prejudices, he soars in spirit above the political limitations of Hellas and Judea, to form out of the mingled thoughts of the prophets and the Platonists the first conception of a humane and loving God, Father of all, as whose sons all men are brothers. Here, on the threshold between one millennium and the next, the kingdom of the soul first discloses itself to the eyes of men.

Man has fallen, says Philo, but it is God's will that he shall save himself through self-knowledge and repentance. Make your vows without taking formal oaths. Practise unity and community, deeming all nations of equal worth. Help your enemy when misfortune lays him low. Watch over the woman who has been made prisoner of war ; be kind to slaves, to immature beasts, and to those that are big with young ; deal kindly, even, with the fruit tree. Deliver yourself from matter, shun distraction, seek solitude, renounce sensual love ; then the body will ecstatically perish, while the soul will return upwards to God from whom it came. Have nothing to do

with lawsuits ; avoid the market-place and public
assemblies. Be simple, meek, unruffled ; eschew
wealth and pride. The world is a foreign
country ; heaven is our true home. One who
knows this and acts on it, one who does good
and serves God, is, by the very wording of the
law, a son of God. For God loves the humble
and the meek and exalts them ; his grace chooses
the pious before birth ; through the power of
his Spirit he reveals himself in holy souls, and
leads them by his inner light beyond the bounds
of the human into the realm of the divine.

VI.

Let us suppose that two elderly Pharisees,
sitting in a corner of the common room at the
inn, could overhear the foregoing conversation.
Every word would be an outrage to them. The
mere sight of the interlocutors would be an
offence to their eyes. The Jew from Rome is
dressed in costly raiment ; he is plump and in
good liking ; well groomed too, being clean-
shaven after the Roman fashion. His friend
from Alexandria is of bland aspect, with kindly
eyes. The Pharisees are lean and hungry men,
lank, grim of visage, white-bearded ; and their
eyes flash as they listen to the talk of these Jews
who are neither hot nor cold—for a Pharisee

hates a Laodicean even more than he hates an unbeliever.

The recreant elders who had translated the word of God into an infidel tongue had been fellows of that ilk, revealing to the heathen the story of the covenant the Lord had made with his chosen people. A deadly sin ! In their schools the Pharisees teach that he who reads a heathen book, were it but one, will be cut off from the life everlasting. Greek is for slaves, not freemen. The writing of the Septuagint version was the beginning of the second period of decay. God has punished this treason, and that is why the Jews are slaves to-day. Coming in their ships, these apostles of a heathen enlightenment bring perilous customs into the Holy Land, even to the very steps of the temple.

The soul ? We have a doctrine of the soul, too ! But to mortify the flesh would lay an axe at the root of our national energies ! Be fruitful and multiply ! These mealy-mouthed strangers ! How many children have they engendered ? The view that revelation is something which concerns only the innermost recesses of the soul, the injunction that we should despise the world of the senses—does not such teaching make light of Israel's glorious past, endanger Israel's glorious future ? In these troublous times, when we are under the Roman yoke, it behoves us to defend with our very lives the spirit of our fathers, the doctrine and the law which even Rome cannot take from us !

Have we ever hesitated to risk our lives in this cause ? Pompey was only able to conquer the Holy City because the besieged were too pious to defend themselves on the Sabbath day. In those times the Jews were a united people, among whom the spirit of the Maccabees was still living. Thanks to Herod, that spirit is no more !

The two elders, crouching in the corner of the common room, talk of Herod the Great, who was still alive when they were boys. King Herod had been an Idumean, a man of sin, little better than an unbeliever. He had betrayed the Holy Land to Cicero the consul, and brought Pompey and Crassus to besiege Jerusalem. Herod, son of a slave, had poisoned his father and his brother, that, by an outpouring of treasure, he could buy the kingly title from the Roman adventurers—and in the end he lost this title. What had his reign profited Israel? True enough, he had regained a great extent of territory, as far as the Anti-Lebanon, as far as the confines of Syria and Arabia, almost renewing the realm of David. But, far from renewing the faith of David, he had shown all the vices of Absalom, had sent gift upon gift to Rome, gratifying the heathen with temples, theatres, and baths ; subsidising Roman gladiatorial shows

even in far Phœnicia ; actually celebrating such
shows on the confines of the Holy City itself ;
thus, barbarian that he was, wooing the favour
of the pagan world and earning the contempt
of his own people ! No one would forget that,
at the cost of millions of drachmas, he had
rebuilt the temple, had gilded the pinnacles,
had covered the hilltop with marble, had set
up folding gates made of Corinthian brass, had
had the curtain of the Holy of Holies woven of
byssus yarn. None the less, he could not gild
his crimes, or weave a web that would hide them
from the sight of men. He might send three
hundred beasts for the sacrifice, but the blood
of the five-and-forty Pharisees, members of the
Supreme Council, whom he had put to death,
still cried against him from the ground. Slave
and flatterer of Rome, he had affixed the golden
eagles of Rome above the great gate, and though
they had soon been removed they had left a
mark which neither the rust nor the rains of
half a century could efface.

Because he had builded a temple and because
he had many wives, he plumed himself on being
the second Solomon ; because Cleopatra had
sent him four hundred retainers, and because he
kept Druses and Teutons as bodyguard, he looked
upon himself as a second Cæsar. Because he had
eunuchs and soothsayers, minions and spies ;
because he played the orator ; because he gave

4

his children Latin names ; because he was married ten times over and begat eleven children—he believed himself to be the father of his country !

Was it to be wondered at that, when Herod died, the whole country had flamed up in revolution ; that here, there, and everywhere soldiers had crowned themselves kings and fought with one another ; till at length those who loved peace had sent to Rome, joining with the Jewish emigrants there in beseeching the emperor that he would restore order, would drive out these false kings? An appeal to the heathen ruler against Jewish upstarts ! Augustus must have smiled inwardly, even though for the sake of appearances he kept a straight face, when in the temple of Apollo he acceded to the petition of eight thousand of the children of Israel, and granted as a boon the very thing he would fain have done on his own initiative. Divide and rule had ever been the motto of Rome. The emperor split Palestine into five parts, giving one of these petty portions to each of Herod's sons, who assumed the proud name of tetrarch—except for Judea, which became a Roman province, so that the governor, in his fortress overlooking the temple, held the heart of the land in his grip.

These two elderly Pharisees could not free their minds from thoughts of the evil plight of their country, though it was one which time might have made familiar. To look before and after is natural at the time of Passover. For we are still the chosen people ! Since the days of Mattathias, for two hundred years and more, the onyx stone has ceased to shine in the high priest's breast-plate, the onyx that aforetime denoted God's presence when sacrifices were offered up. Whence shall deliverance come ? In this city of Jerusalem every thing is curbed, watched, menaced. The standard of revolt must be raised elsewhere, in the north ! Galilee ! There lies our hope ! There, in the land tainted with heathenism, the zealots are waiting and working. Once before, in Galilee, there were ardent youths determined to break the yoke of slavery. Had not the mere proclamation that the people was to be numbered been enough to stir Judas the Galilean to revolt ? " A numbering of the people is wickedness !" he exclaimed, and assembled a troop of enthusiasts. The revolt was against Rome, but also against the Romanising Jews, against Herod most of all, against wealth and worldly power. " No Jew should acknowledge a master ! We are a free people ; God is the chief of our State ; the law of Moses is our constitution. Our God helps those only who help themselves ! We are dagger-men ; we are sicarii !"—With such cries, having armed themselves from the secret arsenals in Galilee, they rushed forth to encounter the legions of Varus.

The failure of that revolt served only to increase the flame of passion, which has glowed ever since in the sons of the slain. They are waiting; they are waiting; making ready in secret to meet force with force. They are men of another metal than the so-called saints who frequent the banks of the Jordan, hoping to bring back the lost realm with prayer and gentleness, with the waters of baptism. From Galilee, from Galilee alone, can deliverance come.

VII.

Behind the golden roof of the temple, the sun has been sinking towards the western sea. Its last rays are shining on the temple of Jupiter at Cæsarea, a temple built by that same King Herod who had lavished so much wealth on the Jewish temple in Jerusalem. The setting sun shines as of old, and the thoughts of those who worship in the temple of Jupiter do not differ much from the thoughts of their fathers who first worshipped there. Men's faith has cooled somewhat since the power of arms attained such unexampled heights, since a worldwide empire rose out of the Mediterranean, and since mortals became as gods. Zeus, Jupiter, and Jehovah have surely grown old, seeing that men must vie one with another for their grace, brother ranged against brother. In Rome, in Alexandria, and here in Palestine, sect wars against sect. No longer does a clear and unambiguous message make its way into the heart of the seeker. In all places, in all tongues, in all religious books, the maxims by which our fathers guided their steps have lost their cogency. Authority is shaken, tradition despised. People no longer dread the lightning, even though it have power to smite them to the ground ; no longer does the sun arouse an impulse to worship ; the images of the gods have become familiar, and ever stronger grows the longing for a faith in invisible gods. Old, very old is such a longing—shrouded in the mists of time.

In great transitions, like the twilight now spreading athwart Jerusalem, in a hundred gradations of the spirit, like those characteristic of the light now fading on Palestine between the eastern hills and the sea, moves and sinks the curve of the old faiths, while there looms through the gathering darkness one star of wisdom after another, gleaming down upon the world of men. Philosophy shines forth when the fires of the gods pale ; yet every school of philosophy tries to confute all the others ; philosophers wrangle, instead of seeking to harmonise their thoughts. Is there still a pure doctrine in the world ? Which is the more arrogant of the twain : the keen-witted stoic, an ascetic wrapped in a beggar's mantle, who believes in destiny and none

the less strives ; or the gentle epicurean, passive
and devoid of illusions, a jester in the halls of the
rich, glad in the quiet enjoyment of such good
things as life may bring ? Both of them preach
brotherliness, enjoin upon us that we should care
for whose who labour and are heavy laden,
urge that the hardships of slavery should be
mitigated. Render unto the State the goods
and services which the State demands, and it
will reward us according to our merits. But
the kingdom of heaven is open to all, without
distinction of deeds or power ; it is open, in
especial, to sufferers and repentant sinners.

Philo tells us that the source of evil is within
the human breast ; the flesh, he says, is sinful,
and the body is the prison of the soul ; all men
are equal in the sight of God, and all of them
thirst to find their eternal home in God, their
father. How closely akin are these teachings
to those of Hillel, the great Pharisee of two
generations ago, a model of good behaviour.
All he had, he had given away, in accordance
with his own precept : " If thy enemy fall, thou
shouldst not rejoice, lest God should see thee,
wax angry, and repay thee in kind. Number
thyself among the oppressed, not among the
oppressors. Never trust thyself, even unto the
day of thy death." He summed his teaching
up in one sentence, which he termed the foundation of Judaism : " What is unpleasing to thyself,

that do not to thy neighbour." Epicurus, living
a thousand miles away, had written : " To do
good is more pleasing than to receive good."

But there was a counterpart ! Hillel's disciples, strictest among the Pharisees, were fond
of the good things of life. God was a severe
ruler, yet at the same time he was a loving
father, governing a good world, forbidding neither
wealth nor pleasure. As his children, we are to
enjoy ourselves. Be watchful to keep the law,
but shun asceticism. Marry when you are
young, that you may beget many children.
Make the most of women and wine, in so far as
the scripture allows, for, in the words of the
Talmud : " Paradise belongs to him who makes
his companions laugh."

But their doctrine, too, was soon riddled by the
objectors. " Why," asked some of the prophets,
" must the invisible, most holy God be appeased
by bloody sacrifices ? Why, if the Jews are
God's chosen people, is God continually visiting
us with affliction, and plunging us back again
and again into slavery ? As a punishment, you
say ? Perhaps it is only because God no longer
has the will to help us. Is not the Greek more
moral and freer than the Jew, enmeshed in the
hundred rules and regulations of Holy Writ."

The spell of proud isolation had first been
broken by the influence of foreign languages,
in the days of the Babylonian exile. Now the

56   PRELUDE

Roman governor talked Greek in conversation with the Jews; the proceedings in the Roman law courts were carried on in Greek; deeds of purchase and sale were written in Greek; priests and laymen, handicraftsmen, and even peasants, must be able to talk to the legionaries. Thus, by slow degrees, the Jews were beginning to find the Greek version of their own scriptures easier to understand than the Hebrew original. The dam had been broken down in many places. In ever-widening streams the western waters were pouring in.

Amid this great relaxation of ancient restrictions, the Pharisees regarded it as their supreme duty to insist upon strict observance of the law, upon strict regard for old custom. Formalism became a passion with them. The Judea of their fathers was sacred in their eyes. The land was sanctified by the levying of the tithe; the seed, by the purging of it from all uncleanness; the Holy City, by the daily sacrifices; while at the summit of the sacred hill dwelt God himself in his Holy of Holies.

If the people would keep the commandments, their faith would bring them freedom once again. The Holy Land would again become a political power. Rome would be overthrown, just as Egypt and Babylonia and Assyria had been overthrown!

But these things could only be achieved by an

exemplary life. The Jews must keep all the feasts and all the fasts ; they must never fail to distinguish between the food that was lawful and the food that was unlawful, between leavened and unleavened bread ; every item of the law of Moses must be fulfilled. Above all, children must be thoroughly grounded in that law. At table, a Pharisee would teach his three-year-old son the ceremonies. The teacher, addressed as " master " and " rabbi," taught the boys the meaning of Holy Writ. He was honoured by all, because he took no money for his services, could cast out devils, could speak in parables, could furnish texts appropriate to every daily need.

The Pharisees idolised the letter of the law, accepting its plain wording without mystical interpretation, doing this at a time when and in a world where a turmoil of conflicting ideas, a state of general uncertainty, prevailed.

They worshipped the letter of the law. On that rock they would split.

VIII.

Again night broods over Jerusalem. The feast of the Passover is at hand. The town is filled with thousands upon thousands of pilgrims, whose hearts are stirring in eager expectation

tinged with awe. What are the thoughts of the
pious as they say their evening prayers? Which
of the prophets do they read by the light of their
tallow dips, while awaiting sleep's caresses?
The visions of Daniel! "And four great beasts
came up from the sea, diverse one from another."
The kingdoms of the world, the realms of Babylon
and of Assyria and of Alexander, all of which
had oppressed God's chosen people, and in turn
had perished. "Behold a fourth beast, dreadful
and terrible, and strong exceedingly; and it had
great iron teeth: it devoured and brake in
pieces, and stamped the residue with the feet
of it." This is Rome, foreseen by Daniel, the
great prophet, companion of Maccabæus the
liberator! Rome would fall, as the three earlier
Gentile dominions had fallen. "And the kingdom and dominion, and the greatness of the
kingdom under the whole heaven, shall be given
to the people of the saints of the most High,
whose kingdom is an everlasting kingdom, and
all dominions shall serve and obey him. . . .
Behold one like the Son of Man came with the
clouds of heaven, and came to the Ancient of
days. . . . And there was given him . . . a
kingdom that all people, nations, and languages,
should serve him."

A Son of Man! Earlier prophets had not
used these words, though the same idea had
vivified their sayings. Since the fall of the great

kingdom of David that had stretched from Lebanon to the Red Sea, all the prophets had known that the mighty new king of Israel would spring from the house of David. " Out of the broken cedar-tree, God shall plant a shoot on Zion." Will the redeemer bring peace, or war ? Some declare that through a great battle, and thus only, will God, starting from Zion, win the promised kingdom for his people. " And it shall come to pass afterwards, that I will pour out my spirit upon all flesh ; and your sons and your daughters shall prophesy, your old men shall dream dreams, your young men shall see visions. . . . And it shall come to pass in that day, that the mountains shall drop down new wine, and the hills shall flow with milk, and all the rivers of Judah shall flow with waters, and a fountain shall come forth of the house of the Lord." So strenuous and so cheerful was the song of the old prophets.

Zechariah, however, looked only for the coming of a prince of peace : " Rejoice greatly, O daughter of Zion ; shout, O daughter of Jerusalem : behold, thy King cometh unto thee : he is just, and having salvation ; lowly, and riding upon an ass, and upon a colt the foal of an ass. And I will cut off the chariot from Ephraim, and the horse from Jerusalem, and the battle bow shall be cut off : and he shall speak peace unto the heathen : and his dominion shall be from sea even to sea, and from the river even to the ends of the earth."

Of like sort had been the prophesying of Hyrcanus, who, a hundred years back, had seen a white bull with golden horns, entering the temple as a great patriarch. As recently as Herod's days there was a psalmist who sang : "Look, Lord, and awaken for them their king, a son of David, at the time thou hast appointed that he may rule Israel as thy servant." Was it not yesterday that the Egyptian sybil had seen the coming of the saviour ?

"But who will the deliverer be ?" Pharisaic precisians were wont to enquire, when evening prayers had been said, "Does he live and breathe, here and now, somewhere in Palestine ? What if once more, as happened when Herod died, false prophets should arise, each claiming to be the Messiah ? There are always plenty of adventurers on the watch for a chance of deceiving the people ! They lead the simple-minded astray with wizardry and magical cures. Galilee is full of insurgents who are ready to do anything that will get them a following. Then there are the Essenes, who sit them down beside the Jordan, weeping into the river, and crying that the kingdom of the spirit is at hand. Woe unto Israel should such a revolutionist or such an enthusiast quote the prophets for his own evil ends, arrogating to himself the powers of the

most High, in order to destroy the law.   A
speedy downfall to such deceivers.   No, no,
the new king of the Jews is not yet in the land
of the living !"

Such are the hopes and fears voiced by the
pious as the night draws on.   Even the enlightened pilgrims from Rome and Alexandria
dream of the promised deliverer.   They have
read Vergil and Horace, and know that these
poets (whose patron was the great Augustus)
had likewise written of a Golden Age, soon to
come, when peace would reign on earth.   Many
declared that fortune would continue to favour
Rome, the ruler of the world ; but Daniel was an
infallible prophet, and his promise would be
fulfilled.   Philo, too, saw in the clouds : " the
divine figure of him who will lead all the Jews to
one place, will intercede with God the Father,
and will secure forgiveness.   Then the destroyed
cities will rise again, the deserts will be peopled,
and the barren lands will bear fruit."

Night broods over the halls of the temple.
The priests on watch sway drowsily betwixt
sleep and waking.   They have forgotten the
Roman soldiers, have forgotten the slavery of
Israel.   Passover is at hand, and their minds
are filled with thoughts of the coming redeemer.

All the sleeping city of Jerusalem is dreaming
of the Messiah.

CHAPTER ONE

CALLING

I.

LYING in the grass on the hillside is a boy, on whom the rays of the morning sun fall aslant as he looks up into the blue of heaven. He might be a shepherd, for sheep are grazing close at hand. All around is still. The hills slope gently towards the valley; there is no sign of other human beings; the lad could sleep soundly and find the flock near by on waking. Yet he does not sleep, and the beasts are not in his care. On Sabbath mornings, he loves to steal away by himself. It is the day of rest, and no one labours in the workshop; he is not needed to help there; betwixt morning prayer and synagogue, he has a free hour. Alone upon the hillside, gazing skyward, he is happy.

For above the hills, and above the clouds, lives our great Father. Of course, he is not there for a boy's seeing. Even Moses saw him but once, though he appeared often enough to the prophets of long ago. Still, in the open countryside, his presence can be felt—a distant nearness. When the wind blows fresh from the sea, so that the old olive trees bow down, and their stems groan in the blast ; when the streamlet, swollen as now by the spring rains, makes its murmur heard more loudly than usual above the bleating of the sheep ; when yonder in the north the white clouds gather round Mount Hermon and hide the summit : then God's voice comes clearly to our ears, for he is a highland god, and does not love the plain.

On this hillside, the boy is amid the mountains, and can see them all. Rounded Tabor is close to him on the left ; away there to the right are the hills of Samaria ; and at the end of the chain is the pointed Carmel, looking as if it might fall into the sea. He has climbed Mount Tabor, but has not yet visited the lake that lies beyond, and does not know if he will ever set foot in the harbour. The place does not draw him. He has listened to numberless tales of ships and of cities ; men have told him of their peoples, that from which one had been stolen away, that to which another was about to return ; echoes linger in the ears of the stripling.

It is lovely up here. There is soft moss to lie upon. The fig trees give so thick a shade that the glare of the sun does not hurt the eyes. There are thorny thickets, but he can avoid their scratches. How near the lark ventures ! It is tame, and not in the least afraid. When the

shepherds come, they do not say a word to him ;
their sheep graze quietly, and are well-behaved.
These gentle sheep, certainly they, too, are
under the loving eyes of the Father, even though
they cannot pray to him. In his sight grows the
fig tree, and his kindly gaze must rest on the lad
in its shade—for he is all-seeing.

Down in Nazareth (whither the boy now
wends his way, for it is time to return)—down
there in the little township of white houses—
they all talk much about God and his temple,
complain that their country has been stolen
from them, and that the heathen rule over the
chosen people. The rich speak more of these
things than the poor ; and the scribes never
stop talking ! What right have such fellows to
intrude into poor folks' houses, to see if they say
their prayers properly ? Father carpenter looks
up anxiously from his plane when one of the
Pharisees comes in, for he knows that the visitor
will faultfind ; will pry into dishes and platters,
and even at the walls of the cottage, to see if
they are clean : will peer into everything to make
sure that the law is being faithfully kept : this
will take an hour or more, and father will not
be able to finish the chair he is making. The
scriptures are splendid ; yet his sisters had fallen
asleep last night when father had been reading
aloud from the Book of Daniel, while mother
was sitting bolt upright in her place.—His

5

thoughts turn to his brothers and sisters, all younger than himself; and to the harsh speech of his father and his mother. He can never think fervently of God when he is listening to them.

When he gets home, he finds that all are ready to go to synagogue. They are in clean clothes, for yesterday mother did the washing. In the dimly lit room of the little plastered hut, the one room, where they sleep and eat together, father is looking for his phylactery. When it has been found, they set out, mother carrying the youngest. The carpenter's bench in front of the door has been cleared away, but the door is left wide open. Who would steal on the Sabbath day, and what is there in the cottage worth stealing?

They pass the well with its arched roof, the well from which his mother brings the water every morning, pitcher on shoulder. They pass many gardens, cool gardens shading the houses of the well-to-do. How luxuriantly everything grows in this upland valley, where water abounds! The ancient cypresses, with their curved tops, grow tall; and scarcely less tall are the date palms. The vines are sprouting famously, and the red-gold of the pomegranates gleams through the interstices in their light-green foliage. But in front of each garden stands a defensive hedge of prickly cactuses; these cruel plants are thickly besprinkled with dust, and almost unrecognisable, so that the unwary passer-by may chance to tear his clothing or his skin. Children hurt themselves on the thorns, and cry with the pain.

The lad notices (for he notices everything which may help to unlock the mystery of the human heart) that some of those who pass by cast envious glances at the roomy pillared houses, richly adorned. He can see no reason for envy ; he has never dreamed of the possibility of living the life of the wealthy. Fresh goat's milk, cheese made from sheep's milk, figs—are not these enough ? Is a carpenter of less account in God's sight than a man of learning ? Why, if tales be true, many of the most noted Pharisees were handicraftsmen ! He would rather sink into the ground than thrust himself forward in the synagogue, into one of those front places where the quality sit.

Still, there was one drawback in being poor. For so long now, father and mother had wanted to make a pilgrimage to Jerusalem ; but to pay the cost of three days' journeyings had been beyond their means. It was a sorrow to them that they could not go. A neighbour's son had gone last year, and had told him all about it. Herod's temple was blazing with gold ; there were huge burnt offerings on the altar ; the high priest was gorgeously dressed ; there was such a bustle in the streets.

Jesus himself had no craving, either for the journey, or for a sight of the temple.

II.

Steps lead up into the long, chill interior of the
synagogue, where father takes his seat with the
elder boys, whilst mother must go to the place
set apart for women. The men crowd in,
talking and disputing as they come. There is
the hazzan, on a high seat at the far end, hard
by the cupboard where the tables of the law are
kept. He calls for silence ; then all stand to say
a prayer. Now he asks who from among the
congregation will read the scriptures to-day. A
man on the front bench rises, a corpulent, white-
bearded man wearing a brightly coloured silk
mantle and a fine shawl garnished with precious
stones. He goes to the lectern, all making way
for him, and begins to read with a chanting
intonation. One of the richest men in the
township, he is learned as well, and no one can
vie with him in almsgiving—of which he makes
a parade. His conduct is irreproachable. He
is always the first to arrive at the house of God,
and the last among those who remain to pray
even after the lamps have been lighted. He is
more scrupulous than any in the observance of
the fasts, brings up his numerous offspring in the
fear of the Lord, gives more than the prescribed
tithe to the temple and the poor, sets a good
example to all. Yet nobody loves him—for,
at bottom, he loves no one.

Discouraged and listless is the poor lad as, standing on tiptoe the better to see between the heads of the congregation, he gazes down the long hall towards the lectern, listening with a bad grace to the familiar words voiced by the fat and self-righteous elder. He has pricks of conscience at his own mood, for the reader has never harmed any one, and has fulfilled all the commandments. He had ordered a table once, and when father had taken it to him he had paid more than the stipulated price. Father had called him a good man. Why should the lad dislike him?—There they were, disputing again, because they were not satisfied with the expounding of the text. They were wrangling about the word " Messiah," whether it meant the same thing as " Son of God " and " Son of David." Louder and angrier grew the voices, and each could quote a passage in scripture which supported his own opinion.—The boy grew hot and cold by turns. He was fain to safeguard the treasures of his innermost being ; to escape from the cramping atmosphere of the synagogue to the freedom of the hillside where the lark came so near, where the brook was his intimate friend, where the clouds scudded overhead, and where between the clouds his vision could pierce the blue vault of heaven.

In the afternoon, the young folk are back again in the chilly synagogue. They squat in

a circle, each with a screed in his hand, following
the text letter by letter with the forefinger. The
hazzan squats in the middle, reading the letters
aloud one after another. Gradually letters become words, words sentences, and all the boys
mechanically intone the passage. This is their
only schooling. If one of them gives any
trouble, the hazzan deals him a blow with the
rod. The lesson is a difficult one, for this
written tongue differs from that which they are
used to speaking. Here in the highlands they
have a dialect of their own, and all Israel makes
fun of them for their Aramaic accent. Such is
the fate of mountain dwellers the world over.
Well, the lesson is finished at last, and the pupils
are free to go where they list.

There is so much to look at in the main street.
It is a high road of the nations. Whatever is
landed at Ptolemais and makes its way to the
interior, to the distant northern hinterland, to
the tetrarchy, to Herod at Tiberias, to the Syrians
in Damascus, must pass by way of Nazareth.
There are camels and packhorses, donkeys drawing carts, soldiers, merchants with their wives
and their slaves. A halt is made here for food
and rest, and the children of the town can get
a good view of everything. They can even pick
up a few scraps of Greek, for in Sepphoris, the
next halting place, only three leagues distant,
there are more heathens than Jews.

Along the eastern road there come to Nazareth Phœnician traders ; scholars from Araby ; and outlandish barbarian adventurers, even more strange of speech, who have been in the service of the tetrarch, and now wish to travel homeward across the sea. Then there are the soldiers, girt with swords, mailclad men who swear and stamp and shout angry orders. The emperor in Rome has recruited them from many lands, fair men and dark, yet lithe and fierce every one. The grown-up Jews turn their backs on the eagles, lest they should have to pay reverence to an idolatrous image ; but the children face about and peep through their fingers, trying to discover what fearful wickedness lies hid in these forbidden pictures.

The coming and going of the heathen, at once alarming and full of great possibilities, is a ceaseless topic of conversation among the Jews. At eventide, when the boy sits in silence beside his father at the cottage door, and the old man chats with one of the neighbours, exchanging complaints that the times are out of joint, much can be gleaned to throw light on what Jesus sees for himself in the street. He stores it all in his memory. So the huge extent of country he saw from the summit of Mount Tabor, that and hundreds of miles more, used to belong to the Jews ! The Romans have taken it away from them, and extort taxes and customs dues in addition. They conquered the temple with fire and sword, and even (so it is said) forced their way into the Holy of Holies. That was but a few years ago. Then came one of Herod's slaves, a handsome fellow, Simon by name ; he burned the king's palace in Jericho. A shepherd, a giant, strong as Moses, had crowned himself and taken up arms against the Romans.

All these risings had been put down.

III.

Of a sudden, Nazareth and Galilee, which had been wont to tremble at the turbulence of the bordering regions, develop a revolt of their own. In Gamala, which is a league or so from Nazareth, a Galilean named Judas has for some time past been getting together a group of stalwarts pledged to effect the liberation of their country. He has a private grudge to work off as well ; for Herod, the tool of Rome, killed his father, and Judas seeks vengeance. He himself is no more than an instrument in the hands of Sadduk, the head of the new party of those who pass by the name of zealots, and have forsworn obedience to Rome. "Our only duty is to God," say they. "We are free. You demand payment of a poll tax ? Why, the prophets threatened King David himself, when he proposed to number Israel ! They make us pay taxes on every stalk of the grain we grow, and customs dues on every flask of the oil we ship. This is worse than covetousness; it inflicts a deadly shame on the chosen people in face of the heathen. If the Pharisees put up with it, they know nothing of the spirit of the prophets; for only through discontent, only through action, can the Messiah, the promised liberator, be found !"

Judas the Galilean and his followers raise the standard of revolt. They rifle the arsenal at Sepphoris, seize whatever Roman money they can lay their hands on, and, with the blessing of the priests, set forth to drive the foreigners out of Palestine. Their army grows rapidly, till the hills of Galilee can no longer contain it. Varus, the Roman commander, hastens south from Syria, with legionaries who outnumber the insurgents by five to one, and the forces of neighbouring princes as allies. He relieves Jerusalem, quells the rising, and crucifies two thousand of his prisoners.—Judas, the leader, escapes.

How the boys thrill when their father and their teacher, amid alternations of hope and fear, tell them of the bold deeds of these Galileans, the early successes and the crowning disaster. Judas, the fugitive, planning a fresh campaign somewhere in the wilds of Lebanon, becomes their hero. After a time they are saddened by the news that the Romans have captured him,

and that he too has died on the cross. He has
been martyred for his nation. The Jews sing
the praises of Judas, who perished for the sake
of freedom, and in the attempt to avenge his
father and many others. The place of cruci-
fixion, on the hilltop over against Jerusalem,
becomes a shrine. For a while, all hearts glow
with hatred ; soon, however, hope surges up
anew. It has become the political faith of the
Jews that they will throw off the Roman yoke.
Then, and not till then, will the Messiah's reign
begin.

Our thoughtful lad holds his peace while
others talk. Eager for knowledge, he is in
general glad to listen to his elders ; and he
looks at them shrewdly, to learn, if he can, the
real tenor of their thoughts. Should a traveller
from Alexandria pass through Nazareth, and
speak of the great library there, tell of the new
sages in the city at the mouth of the Nile, Jesus
will hearken to every word, and will make the
most of the information which a chance wind
blows into the little town in the Galilean highlands. Some wanderer from Greece may have
given him tidings of the heathen prophet who
taught of old in the streets of Athens, when that
city was still great and powerful ; the wise man
who esteemed handicraftsmen more highly than
school or temple, saying : " One that seeks to
know himself, will always do well, and will

thus win happiness." Such a message would stimulate the boy's imagination, and touch his youthful mind to wonderful issues.

But when he is told to hate the heathen and to despise the Romans, and when for the first time he sees the self-feeling of his nation rise to fever heat—he is unmoved. Are we to suppose that God hates others, because he loves us? Are we so free from blemish, that we can afford to think ourselves better than our fellow men? What matter, that Carmel is now in the hands of the Phœnicians; or that, northward of the Sea of Galilee, Philip, son of Herod, reigns? If we are God's chosen people, does that mean that we need to get possession of so many mountains and so many towns? Is it not enough that the temple is ours? What if the Romans tax us, and make us pay customs dues? The rich have a little less; yet all are fed in the end. Has the heavenly kingdom of the Messiah anything to do with the earthly kingdom of the Jews? If Sadduk and Judas wanted only to establish the kingdom of God, what need to seize the swords which the heathen had laid away in store at Sephoris?

IV.

Revolt goes on simmering for years, will go on simmering for decades; best to think of other things.

Jesus is growing up now. After the Nazarene fashion, his black hair is parted in the middle. He is in vigorous health, for he often roams in the mountains ; and in Nazareth, where he does his share of work at the carpenter's bench beside his father, the air is cooler than it is lower down the valley. The wind blows fresh and the hill-sides are green in this well-watered region. Joseph dies, and at nineteen the eldest son has to share with his mother responsibility for the care of the younger children.

He has no thought of marriage, though the law almost enjoins it, and gives a special blessing to the father of many children. Yet he loves women and children, and they love him in return. He is looked upon as rather a queer fellow, for he is so gentle in his ways, so even-tempered and obliging, never quarrelsome. He is sociable as a rule ; a listener rather than a talker ; giving ear to tales of human destiny, which he ponders in his heart. Ever on the alert for the note of human passion, he discovers, as if with a divining rod, the true motives of others' actions. Above all, he can see the weaknesses that are so often masked by loud, pretentious talk ; but he never shows disdain. Understanding much, he forgives everything ; and people trust him because he never assumes the airs of a judge.

Perhaps they are sorry for this young man

who grasps at nothing for himself, and smiles where others show wrath? The rich invite him to their houses, because he knows the scriptures so well, and because he never thrusts himself forward. He sits with them over their wine, the strong wine that is grown in the mountains. He does not shun feasts, or flee the company of women; he is merry with the other guests.

Still, his favourite companions are persons of his own social standing. At the wayside, or on the steps of the synagogue, he sits among those who are as poor as himself, listening while they talk of their troubles. He seeks out vagabonds, from whom the pious hold aloof; is not loath to talk to harlots; will even consort with the publicans, the farmers of the taxes, whom all others despise. For the Jews cannot forgive one of their number who undertakes to wring from his fellow tribesmen the taxes and customs dues which the tetrarch demands, and out of which he draws the tribute he sends to Rome. Wealth gained by farming the taxes, is despicable wealth. Public money is stolen money. The godly should not be taxed save for the upkeep of the temple.

Why does the young carpenter hold converse with such scum? Every one in Nazareth is sure that he gains nothing by it, and he cannot fail to know that to keep company with publicans

and sinners is regarded as disgraceful. Gradually it becomes a matter of common knowledge
that outcasts flock to him because he never
reviles them, because he listens patiently when
they tell him how they came to choose love or
tax-gathering as a profession, and relate their
fruitless efforts to make a livelihood in other ways
before coming to such a pass. It would seem
that this strange youth has a talent for discovering
the remnants of good that linger on in the worst
of malefactors, even when they themselves are
unaware of it ; that in his presence the froward
open their hearts, and the cruel prove less
unkind.

They are men of unsteady temperament, these
Galileans : now brave, self-sacrificing, enthusiasts
for an ideal ; now timid, backward, discouraged
without cause. They lack self-reliance, and have
grown yet more unstable through the mingling
of their blood with that of their heathen
neighbours, converts to Judaism. Nowhere else
are persons with a disordered mind so rife as in
Galilee ; but Jesus has no fear of the possessed.
He looks on undismayed while the devils rage
within one of these afflicted, and is said to have
succoured some from whom all others had fled
in terror.

Only of one sort of persons does he speak
harshly at times : those who make display of
piety, that they may be seen of men in the market

place ; scribes and Pharisees. The better acquainted any one becomes with the scriptures,
the more obvious is the gulf between form
and substance, between letter and spirit. The
Pharisees were fond of saying : "When two who
sit together are not talking of the law, the seat
is a seat of mockers." Again : "Woe unto him
who, when walking by the way and meditating
upon the law, should pause to say, ' How lovely
is that tree !' or ' How beautiful is that newly
ploughed field !' Such a one has forfeited his
life. Above all, woe unto him who interprets the
law in accordance with his own promptings, and
in opposition to the sayings of those learned in
the law : he shall have no part in the world to
come." What, then, are we forbidden to admire
a palm tree ? May we not look at the earth
when meditating upon God ? Do we need the
key of learning to unlock the purport of the
ancient psalms ?

Jesus knows full well the customs and the
commandments, the laws of priesthood and the
laws of marriage, the history of Israel and the
sayings and doings of the prophets. He is, in
truth, learned in the law, though he has no desire
to be regarded as such.—Why do they go to and
fro in the streets, and send far and wide, to spy
out whether the poor keep themselves and their
houses clean ? When they are asked whether
they will free their slaves in the seventh year,

they answer that they will wait till the fiftieth.
The rich take heavy toll from the poor ; they do
not always leave the gleanings, as the law commands ; and when they exact from the poor the
firstlings of the seven fruits for the sacrifice, and
demand in addition temple taxes of wool, cattle,
and wood—the poor become poorer, but do not
grow more pious.

Jesus thinks he does well to sit by the roadside,
waiting for some one to hire him. God will not
let him starve, so why take thought for the
morrow ? Were it not for his mother, his brothers,
and his sisters, he would go up into the mountains, and live upon milk and figs. There are too
many self-righteous folk here in the town. Even
when they are doing what is good in the sight of
God, they are careful that what they do shall be
done in the sight of men also ; and when they sit
over the Torah their eyes are brighter than when
they are under the stars.

He talks after this fashion to a friend or two.
They listen, and repeat his words to others.
Next feast day, several come in the evening, and
remind him of their recent conversation. He is
sitting at the door of the cottage where, within,
his mother is busied at her household tasks ;
and he listens to the quiet voice of his inner self.
It is easy for him to hang what he wants to say
on texts from the scriptures, for he knows them
well, the older books and the newer. To-night,

perhaps, he will speak of Hillel, the good high priest, who had died when he, Jesus, was a boy. Hillel had taught: "What is unpleasing to thyself, that do not to thy neighbour." The same words were to be found in the book of Tobit. Now there was ruling in Jerusalem a Great Sanhedrim composed of the disciples of Shammai. These men, gloomy and strict, taught : " It would have been better for man, had he never been born."—Was it not a sin to talk like that, when there was sunshine to gladden the eyes, when there were hillsides and lambs to look at, flowers and little children ?

Next day, when two more hearers come, and all squat round him in a circle—listening, as so often before, to the words of a man of the people —he is in the fiery mood of the prophets, and quotes from them sayings that well express his own thoughts. Isaiah, for instance, who puts these words into the mouth of the Lord : " To what purpose is the multitude of your sacrifices unto me ? . . . I am full of the burnt offerings of rams, and the fat of fed beasts. . . . Incense is an abomination unto me. . . . Your hands are full of blood. . . . Learn to do well." Then he cites the text from Hosea : " For I desired mercy, and not sacrifice." This, he feels, is his own motto.

When they come on the fourth evening, they do not find him. He has sought solitude in the

6

mountains, for his heart is hot within him
against the priests, and he fears to grow hard.
Serenity returns, while he listens to the murmur
of the wind in the foliage. The wild lilies
spread their fragrance on the evening breeze.
Ere darkness hides it from view, he sees far off
in the land of Shechem the mountain top where
the prophets had sat in the days of long ago.

Snuggling down into the grass, he looks up
at the stars, and feels himself clasped to the
heart of the all-loving Father.

V.

The carpenter, the young man learned in the
law, has heard tidings of a fellowship which,
amid the strife of parties, has silently and in-
conspicuously become established throughout
the land. It is made up of persons who do not
strive after reforms or revolutions, national or
local. They do not seek to persuade any by
argument, wishing only to live their own simple
lives as poor folk, clean at heart. The members
of this order of the Essenes now number four
thousand men and women. They are pious
communists who make no attack upon the rich
or the Pharisees, find fault with no man ; yet
they are resolved to realise in their daily lives
what some of the prophets have taught about

brotherliness and neighbourly love. They are
not cloistered monks, but active in various
occupations, as handicraftsmen, tillers of the
soil, shepherds, beekeepers, and the like. Certain
ways of living are rejected as unclean; no member
of the order can be a trader, a seaman, or an
armourer.

Whoever becomes an Essene must give all
his worldly wealth to the community. A member
who earns more than suffices for his own bare
necessities, hands over the surplus to the order.
They exchange one with another what any may
lack. To the poor, an Essene may give alms
on his own initiative, but he may not give
anything to his kindred—for, since property is
communal, the wealth held in common is dis-
posed of by the assembly, in accordance with the
decision of seniority and majority. " Mine and
thine are thine."

These communities, formed at first on the
borders of the desert, have by degrees spread
nearer to the haunts of men. There are groups
of Essenes in the countryside and the smaller
towns, wherever the members can follow the
permissible occupations. Thus when travelling
in any part of Judea they find brethren of their
own order who can supply their needs. All of
them are Jews, though they have no interest
in the political questions which torment and
divide the Jews in general, though they care

nothing about questions of State, and little
enough about the temple.

They are believers, and yet not orthodox, for
they do many things that are forbidden by the
law. Having risen early, and spent an hour
before sunrise in meditation, they greet the
sun with a prayer to this source of pure light.
After dark, they will not talk of God, holding
that only when light prevails is it proper to
mention the embodiment of wisdom. At the
midday meal, a communal repast, before which
they bathe and put on white linen, one person
only may speak at a time. They abstain from
flesh and from wine, living on a diet of bread,
vegetables, milk, honey, and fruit. Cleanliness
and the plentiful use of water seem to them
more important than formulas. They offer up no
sacrifices; with one exception they take no oaths;
they fast often, and keep the Sabbath so strictly
that they neither touch household utensils nor
attend to the most elementary needs on the day
of rest. Guided by traditional methods, they
study the magical powers of stones and plants ;
they make use of charms and cast out devils ;
they interpret dreams and foretell the future.
Inasmuch as they are known to be free from
covetousness and to have subdued passion, they
inspire general confidence, and people often
ask their counsel.

The duties of marriage and propagation having

been fulfilled in youth, in maturity most of them are celibates, and they recruit their ranks by bringing up the children of others. Their community is divided into four grades, the brethren and sisters being initiated by slow degrees. The only oath they permit is one of secrecy. Every Essene must swear never to reveal the inner mysteries of the order or the names of the brethren. One who breaks this oath, or any of the greater commandments, is expelled, and, as an outcast from the order, will die conscience-racked—though for pity's sake he may be allowed to rejoin when on the point of death. No private possessions, no war, no anger, no violence ; love of enemies, meditation, fellow-feeling ; few ceremonies : such are the means by which the members of this League of Virtue free themselves speedily from the bonds of matter—for the soul is immortal, and is lured as by a sorcery of nature into the prison-house of the body. When released by death, it joyously soars aloft. Such, at least, is the destiny of the pious, whose souls fly upward into a world of light. But the souls of the wicked pass down-wards under the earth, to a realm of wintry darkness and unceasing torment.

From the shores of the Dead Sea, this sect has spread into Galilee, without missionary effort, by the gentle force of example. Jesus takes note of this, and keeps close watch on the men who

fulfil so many of his innermost thoughts. Yet
he does not join their ranks. It is good that they
pray to the sun, even though such prayers are
unlawful and heathenish. Better still, that they
renounce money and the use of weapons. Best
of all that they offer up no sacrifices. But why
do they fast more often than the law commands?
Why do they abstain from wine, forbid cheerful-
ness at board, and reject the pleasures of music?
Why do they shut themselves apart, and inaugu-
rate new mysteries? Professing love for their
neighbours, why should they shun their fellow
men? Akin though the doctrine of the Essenes
is to the tenets that are shaping themselves in
his own mind, he cannot enter their community.

Now it is bruited abroad that a man has
appeared at the edge of the wilderness, hard by
the Jordan, preaching repentance. Instead of
circumcision, he urges baptism with water, to
cleanse body and soul. He has shaggy locks and
a flowing beard. His raiment is of camel's hair,
and he wears a leathern girdle about his loins;
he is lean with fasting and with prayer, burning
with faith; and he utters dread warnings to the
people.—According to the popular voice this was
Elijah, who had once dwelt upon Mount Carmel
in a cave, whence at times he came forth to make
kings and unmake them. Legend declared that
this prophet had never died. One day he would
come again, to deliver Israel.—He has come at

length, Elijah with all his terrors, and the day of vengeance is at hand.

His name was John. From early youth, his parents' vow had devoted him to abstinence, and to a life in the wilderness, close to which he had been born. In that part of the world, the arid, sandy hills and the watered places green with vegetation pass one into the other almost without transition. From the river bank to the desert may be only a step, or at most an hour's walk. The wilderness, there, is but an outlying chamber at the end of a great house. In Jerusalem, John was sedulously trained in knowledge of the law, the design being to make him a priest, following in the footsteps of his father. At length, however, he fled from the school where what they taught him seemed too little or too much. Away from town and rabbis, away from the world of men, back to the wilderness whose solitudes had called to him in his boyhood.

He may have been in touch with the Essenes, though he never entered their fellowship. Like them, he lived a life of poverty and abstinence; like them, he fasted long and often : yet he did not join in their activities or share in their communal discipline. Long years went by before he found himself, and became fully aware of his mission. There was a conflict in his nature. The storms of a questioning disposition, the yearnings of a mystic, drove him towards the

self-absorption of an anchorite; but his imperious
longing to utter a call to repentance brought
him back, in the end, into contact with other
men.   Where the Dead Sea borders on the
parched Arabian wastes, where there is no food
even for beasts of prey, and where the recluse
must seek shelter in rocky caverns, the hardy
John lived upon locusts which he roasted after the
Oriental manner, and upon the honey gathered
by wild bees from the sparse flowers.   Had there
been four-footed creatures to hunt, he had neither
a hunter's knife nor a hunter's will.   His musings
were of God's wrath.   This was the region where
Sodom had bloomed, and had then been fearfully
destroyed.   Jericho was no more than one day's
journey distant.   Would not Jericho, ere long,
share Sodom's fate?

In self-communings and fastings, he had besought God to tell him what he might do and
what he must; but no voice from on high had
answered his supplications, saying: "Arise,
prophet, and show thy face to the people!"
Yet the inner voice gave a clear call, commanding
him to make known to others his conviction that
a crisis was at hand, to warn others against the
vanity of earthly life.   Others?   What others?
His own people!   Perchance Elijah had come
again, in him, to speak through his mouth?—
He shrinks back, affrighted by the shadow his
imagination has conjured up, the shadow of the

great prophet, which dwarfs him in his own sight.
His purpose is strengthened when he recalls the
words of Isaiah : " The voice of one crying in
the wilderness, Prepare ye the way of the Lord,
make his paths straight."

Thus after a period of profound mental
perturbation and self-questioning (in which his
mood varies between sublime confidence in his
own visions on the one hand, and the abasement
of doubt on the other), he goes back at last among
his fellows, to shout aloud the warnings which
had driven him from Jerusalem and the busy
world of men. He returns to Jordan. There,
where the desert mountains fall sheer into the
Dead Sea, and the weary river summons up its
failing powers to rage in eddies and flow round
curves ; there, where David hid from Saul, and
King Zedekiah sought refuge from the Babylonians ; there, where a sandy plain provides meagre
nourishment for a few scattered flocks and herds
—John makes his way to the first houses that loom
in sight. Will the herdsmen run away in fear,
before the savage-looking figure ; or will they seek
to lay him fast and bind him with chains ?
Neither the one thing nor the other, for this is
Judea, where holy men strange of aspect crop up
year after year, seeking always to make good their
claim as prophets by some new quaintness of attire,
some unexampled eccentricity of behaviour.
None will be startled at John's looks in Judea,

where lonely Nature herself flouts all familiar rules, and the wondrous becomes probable.

Two or three herdsmen, then, are the first persons to whom he utters his message. They bring him to the nearest oasis, where all in the village have sight of him and listen to his words. Soon a hundred and more have assembled to hear the stern warning of the half-naked wanderer : " Repent ye : for the kingdom of heaven is at hand." Following the stranger's new commandment, all submit to baptism in the waters of Jordan, confessing their sins.

Jerusalem is eight or ten leagues distant, ever watchful, ever discontented, ever listening with ear attent for some new tune. More likely than not, the man of whom news is brought to the great city is one deceiver the more. But what if, after all, he were Elijah come again ? A man of great stature, bare-footed, clothed with camel's hair, words of warning in his mouth—all these resemble what is told of Elijah. For many, many years, the priests and the Pharisees have been talking about the expected saviour. Can this man be nothing more than an Essene like any other, simply one of those who seek to wash away sin with the waters of baptism ? Night after night, Jerusalem has brooded on the coming of the redeemer. It is natural that the hearts of those who dwell in the city should leap at the tidings of John's advent to Jordan.

Few at first, and then in ever increasing numbers, they go down from the city to see the new
prophet ; the rich filled with curiosity, the poor
uplifted by hope. A little while, and the fame
of the Baptist has spread to every township and
village in Judea. Pilgrims come in troops to
the mouth of Jordan, long caravans of them ; the
faithful and the unfaithful, the weary, the hopeful,
and those who are athirst.

After the lapse of more than a hundred years,
a new prophet has arisen in Israel.

VI.

The carpenter's heart is full of uneasy questionings. News of the Baptist has made its way into
the mountain eyrie at Nazareth. Some of his
intimates have been on pilgrimage to the mouth
of Jordan, and have brought back a strange
tale. With unwonted curiosity, Jesus asks them
to describe John's features, his voice ; to repeat
his words. What is the message which is having
so profound an effect ? The returned pilgrims
tell the carpenter that when they asked the
Baptist, " What shall we do ?" John answered :
" He that hath two coats, let him give to him that
hath none ; and he that hath meat, let him do
likewise." He did not turn away some publicans
who had come to be baptised ; and when they,
too, asked him what they should do, he replied

in friendly fashion : " Exact no more than that
which is appointed you." To the soldiers he
said : " Do violence to no man, neither accuse
any falsely ; and be content with your pay."

Jesus is more and more troubled. An Essene
who is also a preacher ? An anchorite who is
also a teacher ? A pietist who has a message to
deliver to the people ? For the first time, the
carpenter hears of a man who is preaching what he
himself has so long been feeling, and has hitherto
confided only to a few close friends. Against the
sanctimoniousness of the Pharisees, against sacrifices and ceremonies, against wealth and in favour
of equal division among all ? Are not these
Jesus' own thoughts, which this new prophet is
sealing with the waters of Jordan ? Back from
the solitude of the desert into touch with the
fellow men of whose welfare we must always
think ; away from the apathy and the fastings of
the Essenes with their hole-and-corner existence,
back to the multitude ; a reformer ; a man with
a message ! Of late, Jesus himself has so often
pondered the question, " Why dost thou not
stand up to declare before all the world thy
thoughts concerning true beliefs and false ones?"
What he now hears of John makes the matter
urgent. If John, sallying forth from the desert,
utters his warnings to the people, why should
Jesus any longer keep silence ?

The example of the Baptist pricks him on,

stimulates his sense of responsibility, perhaps
awakens his ambition. He joins the next train of
pilgrims going down to Jordan.

There, where the narrow valley is overhung by
limestone hills, along the bank made shaggy with
the growth of rushes and of reeds, he draws near,
three days later, to the throng of men and women
who have come to be baptised. The bare,
fissured rocks give the place a sinister look. The
air is stifling, for the wind comes from the south,
and is tainted with the briny odours of the Dead
Sea. A savage and pitiless region ! The pilgrims
number many hundreds. With them are their
horses and their asses, their children, and the
goats they have brought to provide milk for the
little ones. Poor folk for the most part ; many of
them old, and many of them sick. Not a happy
face among them, though all are filled with
longing. They are squatting on the ground, or
standing, or on their knees, praying. At the very
marge of the river, where there is a flat space,
Jesus catches sight of the Baptist.

Wearing a ragged cloak (for the thorns have
torn it to tatters), John is there ; a tall, lean figure,
unkempt ; and he speaks in menacing tones. He
does, in very truth, look like Elijah, the preacher ;
and all his warnings lead up to the same exhorta-
tion, " Repent ye : for the kingdom of heaven is
at hand." Close by stand some who seem to be
his disciples. Every now and then, the Baptist

takes one aside for a brief space ; then leads him down into the river where it shallows, and pours over him a bucketful of the yellowish-grey waters of Jordan.

Now there is a stir in the crowd. All turn their faces towards the west to watch some new-comers descending into the valley by the road from Jerusalem. Jesus is one of the first to recognise who they are. They are priests and Levites (Pharisees all) numbering a dozen or more on the way to see what they can make of the miracle-monger. As they come down among the rocks they seem uncongenial to the crowd of poor folk on the river bank. In part, no doubt, it is because the townsmen are much better dressed than the multitude, though they have not come in festal attire. Above all, however, it is their manner which repels. They look coldly sceptical, for they have been sent to examine into these alleged wondrous happenings within a day's march of the city. A council has been held in Jerusalem. Enquiries must be made. This flocking together of the common people cannot be allowed to continue unheeded. The Baptist is reported to have been railing against property. Pilate has been asking questions.

With surly deference, from force of habit, the common herd of pilgrims makes way for the quality, so that the men from Jerusalem are soon

face to face with the Baptist. His eyes flash as he encounters their chill scrutiny. When they question him, every answer conveys a challenge, so that almost from the first he seems accuser rather than accused. Meanwhile the encircling pilgrims form an audience.

"Who art thou?" asks the eldest of the newcomers.

John, who senses the underlying import of the question, gives an answer which is an avowal:

"I am not the Christ."

"What then, art thou Elijah?"

"I am not."

"Art thou a prophet?"

"No."

"Who art thou, then, that we may give an answer to them that sent us? What sayest thou of thyself?"

There is a pause, tense with expectation. As yet the Baptist has not let his voice ring out. Jesus, who is one of the circle of onlookers, feels that John will thunder the next answer, and like thunder it comes:

"I am the voice of one crying in the wilderness, Make straight the way of the Lord, as said the prophet Isaiah."

"Why baptisest thou, then, if thou be not the Christ, nor yet Isaiah; if thou be not a prophet?"

"I baptise with water. But one mightier than I cometh, the latchet of whose shoes I am

not worthy to unloose ; he shall baptise you with
fire."

A tremor passes through the waiting crowd.
They breathe more freely, because he has
successfully answered the priest's questions : yet
they are uneasy, seeing that he has spoken of
the Messiah, and has declared that he himself
is not the Messiah. The Pharisees exchange
glances. Not thus, they feel, will they break
down his defences. One asks, therefore, why
he does not go to Samaria, or some other heathen
land. There he will find many who need to
repent. Then John's anger breaks forth more
fiercely than before :

"O viper's brood, who hath warned you to
flee from the wrath to come ? Think not to say
within yourselves, We have Abraham to our
father. I say unto you that God is able of these
stones to raise up children unto Abraham.
And now also the axe is laid unto the root of the
trees : therefore every tree which bringeth not
forth good fruit will be hewn down and cast
into the fire."

" We have heard enough," say the priests and
the Levites, as they turn to go. More than one
of them, perhaps, has fear in his heart, and on his
homeward way he ponders the words of Isaiah :
" Therefore is the anger of the Lord kindled
against his people, and he has stretched forth
his hand against them and hath smitten them :

and the hills did tremble."—The multitude, left encircling John on the river bank, is silent. These common folk do not dare to applaud the Baptist's utterance, much as they would like to, for he has threatened the rich and the powerful. Without saying a word, they beset him more closely than ever.

One, however, stands apart. He has barely heard John's last anathema, for his ears and his heart have been filled with what was said just before, with the Baptist's declaration, "One mightier than I cometh." As in dreams our thoughts move slowly to and fro, fade into oblivion and quicken into life by turns, so in the carpenter's slumbering consciousness do the Baptist's words ebb and flow—to vanish when reverie ceases, and Jesus' mind is fully awake.

Next day, it is his turn for baptism. He tells John his name, dwelling place, and occupation; perhaps more. As for confession, he can think of nothing to confess. True, penitence and prayer are customary with him as with others. Because he loves God, he has conviction of sin; though it is only as a general sense of wrong-doing, for he has no particular sins to relate. Were he to tell John of the only thing for which conscience pricks him at times, the ill will he bears the priests, he would imply that the Baptist's own feelings are sinful in this respect. He is content, therefore, to say little, while

7

studying close at hand the bold fanatic, who
seems a prophet but will not style himself one,
who proposes to begin a revolt against power
and pelf but will not leave the edge of the wilderness. Near in body yet aloof in mind, admiring
yet critical—such is the attitude of Jesus towards
John.

The Baptist's scrutiny of the carpenter is no
less keen. Though the newcomer is but a poor
man, and of quiet bearing, there is something
kingly in his aspect. The gentleness of Jesus'
voice and manner, the innocence of his demeanour, the tranquil gravity with which he
asks for baptism, seem to John (who has looked
into many hearts) to be sustained by a hidden
self-confidence. Whence does a village carpenter derive this? Does the Nazarene himself
know? The two men keep their thoughts to
themselves, however, and go down together into
the river.

There they stand side by side, waist-deep in
the tepid, sluggish, yellow waters of Jordan;
John and Jesus, naked both; John, more than
common tall, wizened, bony; Jesus well-formed
and slender, in the full bloom of young man-
hood; John, with hair and beard long, straggling,
and unkempt; Jesus with neatly smoothed
locks; John the lord of the desert beside Jesus
the lover of gardens; John the anchorite and
fanatic beside Jesus the poet and dreamer. Is

it not already implicit in these two contrasted natures, that it should be the man of delicate frame who bends his head, while the other, the rough-hewn ascetic, should be the one to lay on hands and pour the waters of baptism? John thinks of his office; Jesus, of his Father.

Then, as Jesus comes out of the river, cleansed from the sins he has never committed; still uneasy, since, as far as he himself is concerned, the rite seems unmeaning; amazed, rather than relieved; perplexed by the shifting images of the water, the Baptist, and the multitude—when he draws apart from the others, and stands with eyes closed, striving to regain composure— suddenly flashes appear before his eyes, he sees a vision, hears a voice. It seems to him that the heavens are opened, that a dove flies down, as if to bring him a message. A strange voice speaks to him in his heart, saying: " This is my beloved Son, in whom I am well pleased."

Terrible moment! That was his Father's voice! He has heard it before, many times: in the murmur of the rivulet; in the sheen of the stars; in the babble of children. Then it was wordless, a whisper, a feeling. Now it is articulate, though gentle, talking to him in his own language, calling him Son.

Seized with horror, Jesus flees from the multitude and the Baptist, far away into the desert.

VII.

In the desert, next day, he comes to himself
after a long trance. Slowly, very slowly, the full
memory of what has happened returns ; but his
bewilderment persists, and his spiritual distress
is intensified by solitude. Never before has he
seen the desert, and it is hateful to him. All that
from childhood upwards has spoken to him of
God—flowers and running waters, the birds and
the beasts, the stream of human endeavour—
is lacking here in this desolation of lifeless sand,
rising in hillocks and sinking in furrows, crumb-
ling betwixt his fingers. Here, he cannot pray.

Yet God's voice has called him. Was it but
yesterday ? It resounded in his heart, strange
and remote, naming him Son. The voice spoke
when he was coming away from the baptism
which had brought so much distress. The voice
spoke when he had the vision in which a dove
flew down to him from heaven. Alone, with
naught but sand beneath and sky above, he now
asks himself what this voice can betoken. Time
and place count for nothing here. His work
and his home are far away ; he is out of touch
with the familiar things of daily life. For days,
for weeks, he turns the question over and over
in his mind, resolved to dwell in the wilderness
till understanding dawns.

Was it a summons from the heavenly Father?
If so, surely the voice would have spoken more
plainly, as it had spoken to the great prophets
of old. If God's purpose had only been to
strengthen him in his course, why was the message
so phrased as to fall in with his own most secret
thoughts? For, in very truth, all the time on
Jordan's bank he had been comparing himself
with the man who was baptising there, wondering whether John's aspect and John's words
could really be pleasing to the Lord. In his
musings, he had fancied himself in John's place,
had thought how differently he would himself
perform the rite of baptism. Had he not felt
twinges of jealousy, to see the multitude swarming
round the haggard anchorite, who probably
had no better insight into the faith than himself?
Moreover, when he was coming up out of the
river, had he not asked himself why he, un-
constrained by the law, should for the first time
have put himself into the hands of another?
God had been watching him, then; God had
known what was hidden from mortal eyes!
But why had the Father chosen this moment of
supreme moral weakness in which to send a
first direct message, in which to strengthen
him!

There must be more meaning in it than that.
The voice must have given him a charge. Was
he to follow the Baptist's example; preach

repentance ; wander through the country, teaching ? Was he bidden to forsake his handicraft,
his birthplace, his nearest and dearest, the
peaceful life of home ; to take up a career of
action ? Was he to do everything in John's
way—only in John's way ? Was not John merely
setting up a new ceremonial in place of the old ?
Why this asceticism and flight into the wilderness ;
why these fastings and this mortification of the
flesh ? Were not such injunctions akin to the
sacrifices which the Baptist himself rejected ?
Why did he talk of punishments and disasters,
instead of dwelling on the Father's grace ?
What was the use of trying to force people to their
knees by frightening them with threats ? Fear
does not strengthen faith. It would be more
pleasing in God's sight were he to raise them up,
the poor and the heavy laden who were kneeling
round him on the river bank ; to visit them one
by one in their homes or work places ; then to
assemble them near their villages in a meadow
or on the hillside, and in quiet words to tell them
about the feelings and the wishes of the Father
of us all !

Nevertheless, how great John was ! How the
lightnings of his gaze had flashed round those
priests ! How he had emptied the vials of his
scorn over them, speaking of Abraham's children,
and implying that a converted heathen could be
as good a man as they ! He did not urge a

fight against the Romans ; he did not preach revolt. Self-communing, poverty, humility — that was the essence of his teachings. He would not accept the name of prophet.

"One mightier than I cometh !" Suppose that Jesus had himself been chosen ? Suppose that it was for this reason that his Father's voice had spoken to him after the baptism ? What ? Was he to succeed, perhaps to supplant, John ? With horror he tried to thrust away the thought which so persistently returned, feeling that to supplant the Baptist would mean the betrayal of the man who, yesterday, had laid kindly hands on his head.

In this state of mental anguish, he begins to fast, as John had fasted in the wilderness before him. It is his first trial at prolonged mortification of the flesh, for never has he known so fearful a perplexity ; never before has he needed a test, a sign, as he needs them now, when he has had a sign which he does not understand. Day by day, the nerves and the senses of the fasting anchorite grow weaker, and day by day his thoughts become more lucid. His mood alternates between exaltation and exhaustion. Now come visions such as he has never known, or never heeded, before. Hunger weakens the resistances of his body. Thereupon temptations assail him, striving to catch him unawares.

The longing to be singled out, to be chosen,
spurs him forward to make unwonted demands
on himself; his self-confidence grows hour by
hour. A voice within him asks mockingly why
he does not command the stones to become
bread, even as John had said that of the stones
God could raise up children. He refrains from
the attempt, for another voice speaks, saying :
" Man shall not live by bread alone, but by
every word of God."   Waking from a half-
sleep, he is convinced that he has been
tempted of the devil, whom he has often seen
raging in the possessed ; and he arms himself
anew.

Then, in a dream, he feels himself carried to
a pinnacle of the temple, uplifted above all the
people. There the seductive voice of ambition,
the same voice that had beguiled him when
he was contemplating the Baptist, adjures him
once again : " If thou be the Son of God, cast
thyself down from hence, for it is written :
' He shall give his angels charge concerning
thee, to guard thee. And on their hands they
shall bear thee up, lest haply thou dash thy foot
against a stone.' "—How alluring is the golden
roof at his feet, and the wide city which he has
not yet seen with his bodily eyes ! Could he,
but for a moment, become prophet in Jerusalem !
—Then he hears the promptings of the better
voice, which makes answer within him : " It is

also written, 'Thou shalt not tempt the Lord
thy God.' "

Yet, wave after wave, fresh temptations come.
He yearns for home. What has become of the
quietude which filled his mind when he dwelt
in his Father's peace, had nothing to refuse,
and coveted nothing? Why should he become
a fighter? The fever of imagination returns.
The solitary in the wilderness, fainting with
hunger, must resist a third assault of temptation.
This time he feels himself borne to the summit
of a lofty mountain, whence he can see the kingdoms of the earth ; and the devil says to him :
" All these things will I give thee, if thou wilt
fall down and worship me." Thereupon Jesus
summons up his forces, and cries out : " Get thee
hence, Satan : for it is written, ' Thou shalt
worship the Lord thy God, and him only shalt
thou serve !' "

With his own voice ringing in his ears, he flees
from this region of terror, even more distraught
than when he had entered it ; haunted by the
vision of horrible faces ; agonised, despairing.
He will return home, back to his own cottage,
back to the carpenter's bench, back to the little
village on the western slope of the mountain,
back to the peaceful world where grass grows
on the hillside.

As he draws near to the river, he is determined
to make a circuit, and thus avoid the region of

John's ministrations. But his progress is stayed
by a multitude in confusion, as if running away
from a stricken field. Far off he sees a company
of soldiers, marching eastward. With anxious
forebodings, he asks some of the fugitives what
has happened. They are amazed that Jesus
has not heard the news. The Baptist has been
taken prisoner ! Herod Antipas, the tetrarch,
has sent hirelings to seize him ! There go the
soldiers, still visible in the light of the setting sun !
They have with them John, heavily fettered, on
his way to a prison whence the only release will
be death !

The sign ! Jesus stands petrified. God has
decided, and the conflict that has been ringing in
Jesus' mind is stilled. He may, he can, he must !
That is why his Father's voice has spoken ! That
is why he has been tempted of the devil ! All
to strengthen his weakness ; to steel him in the
resolve to follow in John's footsteps, to take
John's place ! " One mightier than I cometh !"
His gentle features stiffen into a mask. Those
who have given him the tidings, look at him in
astonishment and alarm. Some who have known
him of old, turn away from him in distress, for
his expression seems to them stubborn and
arrogant.

When he has shaken off the immobility which
had seized him at the first hearing of the news,
and when he has resumed his homeward journey,

his thoughts enter a fresh path. For the first
time in his life he makes plans ; asks himself how
he shall begin, and where ; recalls the characteristics of the few close friends he has, and
wonders whether this, that, or the other of them
will have faith in him. As he journeys northward, alone, comparisons between what the
Baptist did and what he himself will do force
themselves into his mind. Had John been wise
to revile the Pharisees ? Would it not be better
to avoid offending them ? With kindlier phrasing,
as much and more might have been achieved,
without arousing the secular authorities to
action.—He goes on to think about his daily
work as carpenter. Will his brothers be able to
do without him ? Which of them will best
replace him in the handling of the tools of his
trade ?

When he gets back to Nazareth, he is told that
his mother and his brothers are away at Cana,
three leagues to the north. There is a marriage
feast. Will not he go thither too ? The prospect
draws him. He thinks of the bright dresses and
the lively sounds. The cheerful customs of his
native region exercise their spell. He has been
shaken to the soul by his recent experiences,
and craves for distraction and rest. He goes to
Cana.

The merry-making is at its height. To the
clashing of cymbals and the piping of flutes, the

peasants are singing and dancing as gaily as if
they had never heard of the day of judgment. He
watched them for a while. They are obviously
rather drunk, and yet none of them are now
drinking. Has the wine run short? The wedding
festivities have been going on for three days,
now ; and, not being wealthy people, they must
have emptied their cellar. Are those young
women dancing over there really his sisters?
That man roaring with laughter as he slaps
a thigh, is it really his brother? The new
thoughts with which his mind has been filled are
at war with old associations.

When he draws nearer, and they recognise
him, there is an uneasy silence. They feel that
he is watching them unsympathetically. His
manners are not those of a wedding guest, and
make him somewhat of a kill-joy. He is asked
with a laugh what befell him beside Jordan,
and whether he liked baptism. A second
nudges a third, and points to the spectral
visage that looms over the feast. A fourth,
embarrassed, calls to him that the wine is
finished. Does Jesus know of a fresh supply?
He makes no answer, but stands in silence,
brooding.

His mother, who is seated at the table, and
wants to awaken him from his reverie, says to
him gently : " They have no wine."

Then, when he hears his mother's voice, and when her words convey an appeal to him, the sense of oppression masters him anew. Suddenly he feels himself set apart ; fresh faces lure him, voices hitherto unheard call him, away from familiar surroundings, away from the things which so far have been the elements of his simple happiness. Again his countenance sets into a mask. As if from a great distance, he looks coldly at the mother who bore him, saying : " Woman, what have I to do with thee ?"

A shudder runs among the fuddled guests. His mother turns pale. In the twinkling of an eye, the company is sobered. All stare at the carpenter of Nazareth. They have looked upon him as an eccentric, but have ever regarded him as a good son and a kindly fellow. What has happened to him ? Is he possessed ? What is he looking at so fixedly ?

To Jesus it seems that his soul is strengthened. For the first time, when in the presence of a great number of persons, does he feel himself empowered to influence them, to guide them, to command them. For the first time, he feels himself to be a prophet. He is surrounded by signs, and of these the most immediate is that there is no wine. He, chosen to follow in John's footsteps, must surely be strong enough to turn water into wine ? Did he lack such a power, how could he teach the people ? He cannot help but try his new strength, which no one yet knows him to possess—though he has startled the guests with a foretaste of it when speaking as he did just now to his mother.

With a masterful gesture, such as no one has seen him use up to now, he tells the slaves to bring the six pitchers which are kept for the storage of water, and to fill them afresh. When this has been done, he orders them to draw out some, and bear it to the cook (who knew nothing of the matter). All look at Jesus, and then at the cook ; for he, amazed, stands in the doorway calling to the bridegroom : " Every man at the beginning doth set forth good wine ; and when men have well drunk, then that which is worse : but thou hast kept the good wine till now !"

Once more they stare at Jesus, who has been strong enough, through the wall, to make the cook out there believe what, from within, Jesus has willed him to believe. He must be a wizard !

The babble begins anew, while one alone among the company looks on clear of mind, filled with the insight of the Chosen. So this is the people ; those whom it is his mission to teach ?

Will they follow him, since he has nothing to offer them but thoughts? Gloomy, wrapped in meditation, he leaves the roysterers to their merry-making.

This was the first miracle wrought by the prophet of Nazareth.

CHAPTER TWO

GLAD TIDINGS

I.

" BELIEVE the glad tidings !"

Thus does the stranger's message ring through the great hall, while all stare at him open-eyed—shipmen and traders, craftsmen and travellers, who throng the synagogue. For we are in Capernaum, the haven on the northern shore of the Sea of Galilee, and a halting-place on the trade route from the Mediterranean to Damascus. Hither come the caravans. With them are men learned in the law, and men learned in the wisdom of the heathen ; rich men, too, and men who travel in search of distraction. On the Sabbath, these wayfarers visit the synagogue, to which the dwellers in the city likewise flock, eager for news of the outer world. To any stranger who can read, a Capernaite will proffer a copy of Holy Writ, begging him to read a passage aloud, and to interpret it by the latest light from Jerusalem.

This man, who arrived but yesterday and is holding forth to-day, comes from nearby (so runs the report from one to another). Nazareth is but a day's journey, for one who starts at dawn.

8

Can any good thing come out of Nazareth ?
When he rises and begins to pray, the congregation looks at him in amazement, for he speaks
softly, as if communing with himself ; and when
he mounts the lectern, all can see that he is not
an accredited teacher, for his raiment lacks the
four-pointed fringe which the law enjoins.   Is he,
perchance, a disciple of John, who was seized a
few days ago and cast into prison ?   Are these
baptists forsaking the banks of Jordan to make
their way through the country ?   He seems too
kindly to be one of the baptists ; he does not wear
a hair shirt after the manner of the ascetics, nor
yet the prophet's mantle which many don when
they would fain be taken for a new Elijah ; nor
are his looks and his words gloomy and menacing.

"The time is fulfilled, and the kingdom of
God is at hand : repent ye and believe the glad
tidings !"

This message has a very different sound from
that of the baptists of Jordan.   He does not utter
threats or warnings ; does not urge confession or
baptism.   He explains the old prophecies in
words that touch on the familiar things of daily
life.   Since he does not wear the fringed garment
of the rabbi, and does not teach them out of the
Book ; since he is content, talking to them in
their own vernacular, to tell them in convincing
tones that he who believes may hope—he quickly
wins the confidence of these simple fisher folk and

tillers of the soil, who in their secret hearts are weary of the hairsplitting discussions of the Pharisees. "Glad tidings!" That is something new, and it is something which even a child can understand. He goes on to say that the kingdom of heaven is like a net that is cast into the sea and gathers a multitude of fishes, some good and some bad.

The fisher folk nudge one another and grin, for the parable goes home. They listen all the more attentively when he goes on to speak of a sower, who scatters the seed so that some falls by the wayside, some among thorns, some upon stony places, and some upon good ground. But always the preacher has the kingdom of heaven in his mind ; and not one of the congregation fails to understand him when he tells of the two debtors, one of whom owed much and the other little, and of the talents that were put out on usury, pointing the moral in each case with reference to the great settlement with God when life comes to an end. The women, too, sitting apart behind the grating, listen and nod when he describes the old garments which should not be patched with new cloth, and the old bottles which should not be filled with new wine ; the widow who importunes the judge ; the housewife who turns the place upside down in her search for a lost piece of silver. That is the world as they know it. They have often been wearied by the stereotyped prayers and the sonorous texts of the priests. This stranger is worth listening to ; he seems to be almost one of themselves, though not born on the shores of Galilee. They peer at him through their veils, well pleased with his neatly trimmed beard, with his anointed locks, and with the gentle tones of his melodious voice.

The only ones among his auditors who do not like him are three or four scribes sitting on the front benches. They know directly he begins to speak that he has not been trained for the priesthood. Though he seems well versed in scripture, he certainly has little knowledge of the commentaries, which are quite as important. As long as these self-taught fellows keep to their native villages, they do no harm ; for there no one takes them seriously. But when they become itinerant preachers, the common people are agape, think that they must be wonderful because they are strangers, and cease to pay due respect to the elders of their own countryside. This strolling evangelist has devised a new scheme for making folk listen to him. His preaching is like a wayside conversation, essentially profane. Thus he ensures himself a good reception, and is able for weeks at a time to live in clover at the cost of his dupes.

While they are impatiently awaiting the end of the sermon, while the preacher is using his hands to help out the meaning of his words, suddenly a loud cry is heard in the synagogue. He stops speaking, and looks towards the far end of the hall, where people have drawn away in alarm from a man who has fallen down in a fit. Foaming at the mouth, amid convulsive twitchings, this poor creature shouts : " Let us alone ! What have we to do with thee, thou Jesus of Nazareth ? Art thou come to destroy us ? I know thee who thou art, the Holy One of God !"

Thus does a half-demented man piece together the friendly and the hostile impressions which hundreds have received from the stranger's address. It is as if he had sensed the mute alienation of the few Pharisees, and the tacit approval of the numerous uninstructed hearers. He snaps the tension by simultaneously reviling and worshipping the stranger.

Jesus is profoundly moved. For the first time he is talking openly, to a multitude, of the things he has brooded over so long. The coldness that had mastered him when his mother had spoken to him at Cana, the self-confidence that had urged him to deliver his message to a wider world than Nazareth, had kept him away from home, and had directed his footsteps towards this populous lakeside region. Only for a few moments had he been uneasy, at the outset of his discourse, when the questioning glances of the scholars had troubled him. Then he had

fixed his gaze upon the husbandmen and fishermen, the young people and the women folk,
and in their eyes had intuitively read something
which had taught him how best to appeal to their
understandings and touch their hearts. Now
came the cry of the possessed man, the aspect of
the frightened congregation, the bustle of general
anxiety, to renew the condition of mental distress
which had seized him at the wedding, when his
mother had said to him : " They have no
wine."

With swift strides, he draws near the sick man,
people making room as for a physician. He
kneels down beside the invalid, grips him firmly,
looks at him fixedly, shakes him, and exclaims :
" Hold thy peace, and come out of him !"
Thereupon the patient tosses from side to side,
screams, rolls his eyes, and is again convulsed.
Then, under stress of Jesus' compelling gaze,
thrilled to the marrow by the urgency of an
unprecedented command and by the awesome-
ness of the scene in this holy place, he surrenders
to the new impressions. His limbs relax, his
eyes close, his breathing grows calm. Soon he
opens his eyes once more, and looks up quietly
at the exorcist. He feels that the devil, in whose
existence both of them believe with equal fervour,
quits him even as has been ordered. He believes
this because the stranger compels him to believe
it. The storm has passed, and, assuaged though

still rather weak, he rises to his feet—seemingly
cured.

Hundreds have witnessed the miracle. The
stranger is one of those magicians who can drive
out devils, like the prophets of old. Reverently,
the crowd divides to let him pass. But Jesus
is weary. The joy of preaching, which had
increased while he was speaking, the physician's
fixity of purpose, which had demanded all his
energy to sustain, have vanished ; he flees from
the multitude, shuns the streets, makes his way
out of the town. Not till he has reached the
shore of the lake does he sink to the ground,
lying on the sand among the reeds, striving to
regain his composure.

II.

Green and clear are the waters of the Sea of
Galilee, shimmering in the light of the afternoon
sun, nestling under the mountain side. Capernaum lies in a bay, well protected from the wind ;
a bay containing several towns and villages,
all of which can be seen from this northern
vantage ground. That village to the right, two
leagues away, white and gleaming, with the
tower, is the newly built Tiberias, where Herod
Antipas reigns. Lord of this tetrarchy, by the
name of his capital, and by the temple and the
eagles which adorn it, Herod flatters the Roman

emperor upon whose caprice his power depends. Away to the left, Jordan opens into the lake ; and at the southern end Jesus can imagine, if he cannot see, the spot where the river resumes its southward course to end in the Dead Sea.

Perhaps he is thinking of that southern outlet, of the man who baptised him there, and of how the dread but delightful voice of the Father came to awaken him from the slumber of years. Of Herod, he does not think. Herod is naught to him ; just as Tiberius, the lonely emperor on the isle in a far-off sea, is naught ; just as all the fleeting principalities and powers of this world are naught to him. He thinks of the birds that flutter round him. There is the turtle-dove he knows so well at home ; she, for her part, seems to recognise him, for she comes out from among the bulrushes, hops across the ooze, closer and closer. But the pelican keeps his distance, a big fellow and suspicious, much less inclined to trust men than is the little dove ; the pelican is afraid of the fowler. When the wanderer pushes away the shells, and digs into the sand with the edge of a big one, he soon comes down to black rock. It is basalt, for the region is volcanic. A few years before, there had been an earthquake, in which many thousand persons had lost their lives.

Jesus does not see these things superficially, as most people do. He has a poet's vision, and therefore an eye for hidden resemblances. The hills and the rocks, the river and the castle, the catastrophes of nature and the flower-clad slopes that surround him where grapes and melons are ripening though April is not yet over—all breathe a meaning to him, all give him food for thought. That craggy mountain behind him, how like to Hermon with its caves and spurs and patches of unmelted snow. At the foot of this threatening hillside, the lake spreads its waters as lovely as life itself ; and well does he know the saying of the Lord, who chose this sea as the loveliest among the seven seas of Israel.

Then, as the day darkens, the wanderer sees many boats putting out from shore, to draw the nets, for at twilight the fish come to the surface and the first star that shines in the east is the sign that the Sabbath is finished and that work may be resumed. The fishermen call to one another from boat to boat, draw their nets, empty the struggling fish into the boats, and then row quickly landward, for in these latitudes night comes swift of foot.

When two of them land close by the stranger, they recognise in him the wonder-worker of the synagogue ; and he recognises one of the fishers, for it is Andrew, a disciple of John the Baptist, and Jesus had seen him only a little while ago by the lower Jordan. Andrew makes known to Jesus his brother Simon—for, in accordance with the lax customs of the day, the parents have called one of their sons by a Jewish name and the other by a Greek. When the three now clasp friendly hands, not one of them foresees what will be the upshot of the meeting, nor does Jesus know that in time to come he will himself give this Simon the Greek name of Peter.

Two other fishermen arrive, eager to become more closely acquainted with the miracle-worker. These, too, are brothers; James and John by name. Other men follow them, and one and all put their trust in the stranger. This is not only because he has driven a devil out of a man possessed; the Pharisees have worked that wonder often enough. But his words in the synagogue, coming straight from the heart, have touched the hearts of these simple fellows. Now that it is dark and they must all go home, Simon takes Jesus to his own cottage, asking him to share in the evening meal. Soon, half the population of the little town has assembled outside the door. It is the eve of a festival, and they would like to see with their own eyes this stranger who can heal the sick.

Within, Simon's wife's mother lies sick of a fever. Since he has given them so great a proof of his skill as a healer, they lead him to her, and look at him expectantly. He understands their wishes. Reluctant though he may be to win fame as a miraculous healer, what is he to do?

Behind him, a crowd of onlookers has entered
the outer room ; many of them are peering
through the doorway ; all are waiting. Had not
Moses and the prophets to work miracles before
people would listen to their message ? The old
woman who lies sick believes in him, for she has
been told of what happened that morning in the
synagogue ; she looks up piteously and yet confidently into the kindly face of the stranger.
She longs to be well again, and he wishes to
restore her to health. Both of them have faith
in his power ; and out of this faith, healing power
springs. He stands over her, gazing into her
eyes. The fever is mastered, and she rises from
the bed of sickness.

The onlookers regard him with gratitude and
awe ; but Jesus is filled with fear and secret
loathing that the role of miraculous healer should
be thrust upon him. On the morrow, a multitude
of the sick gathers in front of Simon's door ;
many of them, too ill to rise from their beds, are
carried thither ; some with boils and blains, some
blind, and some stricken with palsy ; all in search
of a cure. He does what he can. Some are
relieved for a long time, others for a brief space.
Many he anoints with oil, others with clay ;
from all he demands faith, as essential to being
made whole. Yet so repugnant are these doings
to him, that he must always constrain himself
to them by calling upon his sympathy with the

afflicted ; and always, when he has worked a cure, he is insistent that the patient shall tell no man. The injunction is disregarded ; the story of his doings is noised abroad, with plentiful exaggerations ; and early one morning, before day has fully dawned, he departs from Capernaum in order to regain his mental poise in solitude.

Nevertheless the common folk, the fishermen and the tillers of the soil, follow him, wishing to hear more of his message. Numbers of women come likewise ; and, first among them, the mother of James and John. Soon they grow accustomed to have him in their company when they are sitting by the lake, mending nets, tarring boats, or cutting oars. Surrounded by these poor people who glance up at him occasionally from their work, squatting on the strand among the shells, in the shade of a few ancient tamarinds, while the sedges rustle in the breeze and the wavelets plash on the shore ; among the un-lettered, the men and women of simple faith, the good—then Jesus is happy ; then the current of his loving thoughts begins to flow in the channel of carefully finished parables, for when he speaks of the kingdom of heaven he need merely point skyward.

How small this great world is ! Every league you come to a new village ; in an hour you can cross the lake ; and yet Jesus needs many weeks, and the summer is well advanced, before he has

visited all the towns and villages that cluster
round the Lake of Gennesaret. He does not
wait for people to come to him, as John did.
He seeks them out. And since his first adherents
continue to follow his footsteps, he is soon
accompanied from place to place by a multitude,
and his fame runs before him.

Among people so religious and in times so
anxious, an itinerant preacher such as Jesus
readily finds disciples, who follow him and help
him. These poor fishermen have little to lose
when they leave their homes. Uncultured folk
scarcely able to distinguish between the kingdom
of heaven and the freeing of Israel upon earth,
but prone to reverie and filled with eager aspirations, they are ready to follow one who brings such
glad tidings, and awakens in them a desire for
richer experiences, a wish to learn many things
which they have not learned in their daily avoca-
tions. Besides, Jesus is a cheerful companion,
enjoys good food and good wine, and does not
tell them to shun the company of women. Youth,
the spirit of adventure, the glad tidings and the
pleasing personality of the man who brings them,
superstition, the hope of reward in heaven—such
are the lures that induce these young people to
follow the new prophet in his wanderings.

People flock together from the valleys and the
mountains, attracted by the fame of the new
physician and wonder-worker, eager to hear his

words. If there is too large an assembly for all to hear him easily, in a village where there is no synagogue, he steps into a fishing smack and makes his friends push off from the shore, on which the congregation gathers. The water carries the words of his glad tidings, the message he conveys in fresh and ever fresh parables, each of which has some pointed application to the narrow circumstances of their daily life; for, in his view, only through parables, only through the power of art, can such teaching as his be brought home to the people. He even ventures to show forth God in verbal imagery, though the Jews are forbidden to make any image of God. He tells his hearers that God is seated in heaven like a king upon the throne, and that the earth is God's footstool; he depicts God as the lord of a vineyard, as a friendly host, as the owner of many slaves.

With the inner mind, he perceives the inaudible echo that comes back to him from the responsive hearts of his uninstructed auditors. When they question him, he answers them; when they bring him their sick, he cures if he can; and then he goes on his way. In front of a house where he takes up his quarters, many gather hoping he will speak to them; at the cross roads he halts to address those who may be there, few or many; and if there be women and children among them, his phrasing is simpler and clearer than ever. His crowning delight is to linger with his

disciples at board ; and to them he gives his full confidence, talking as freely as he used to in Nazareth when a friend or two had gathered to hear him in front of the carpenter's cottage.

The only places he avoids are the larger towns. He never goes to Tiberias, though every child in the countryside has been thither once at least, to gape at its splendours. He keeps away, even, from Taricheae and Sepphoris. Such places, he feels, are the centres of a bustling life, the homes of authority and ambition and money ; those who dwell there will have no ears for his message.

Farther to the south, in Judea, is the great city where powerful priests hold sway, interpreters of Holy Writ, masters of formula. The tacit hostility of the scribes in the synagogue at Capernaum has shown him that men of this sort are his enemies.

Jesus keeps far away from Jerusalem.

III.

The love with which his heart is filled flows over all with whom he is in contact. He has come to share in people's loves, not in their hates ; and he never seeks a quarrel with any one. What he teaches the common folk in his goings to and fro beside the Lake of Gennesaret, is adapted to their intelligence, and would only arouse cultured

doubt in the shrewd minds of learned townsmen.
Simple souls accept it readily, for such men as
these fishers, who must show patience day after
day casting their nets or throwing out fishing
lines from their boats or from the shore, form
a gentle and kindly audience ; they are not led
into temptation by any overwhelming urge to
action.   Nor does he perplex them by talking of
world-wide empire, of power and glory, of the
present slavery and the past greatness of the Jewish
people ; he does not even refer to God's vengeance
and punishments, to God's wrath and requital.

An abundant source of grace springs from the
heart of this loving man ; and his first care is
to direct its waters towards the heavenly Father,
whose gift it is.   Since all are children of the one
great Father—the innocent, the tender-minded,
the unlettered, will understand him most readily,
seeing that they think as little as a child.   He who
has perfect faith in God's goodness, lives under
God's special protection, for God " maketh his
sun to rise on the evil and on the good, and sendeth
rain on the just and on the unjust."   One who
cherishes this faith will soon have the kingdom of
heaven on earth, and will find a treasure in the
field of this world.

Such words are readily understood by the superstitious peasants who sit round the teacher, for
the air is filled with tales of wonder, and the
prophets saw the windows of heaven opened.

Every one of them has heard the tale of the man whose ploughshare turned up a hoard of buried silver ; every one of them has had an unpopular neighbour on whose fields the good rain fell no less abundantly than on his own. They are scarcely aware that, long ago, the prophet Daniel had spoken in like manner of the coming of heaven upon earth ; and still less do they know that in boyhood the man from Nazareth had been wont to lie with an ear buried in the grass, listening for the footfall, feeling the universal presence, of the loving Father he now describes. The simple in spirit believe him because he utters no threats, but brings them glad tidings ; because he discloses a happiness near to their grasp, calling it the kingdom of heaven ; and because, when doing so, he does not, like the Baptist, demand the gnashing of teeth. " Ask, and it shall be given you ; seek, and ye shall find ; knock, and it shall be opened unto you." No priest in the house of God ever spoke such words of consolation to the poor !

Surely he does well to call us brothers, since we all have the same Father ! When our brother wrongs us, should we pay him back in his own coin, demanding an eye for an eye, and a tooth for a tooth, as the Sadducees teach in the great city ? Still, this new preacher gives us a word which is none so easy to follow : " Whosoever shall smite thee on thy right cheek, turn to him

9

the other also. And if any man will sue thee at
the law, and take away thy coat, let him have thy
cloak also." While they are still in a quandary,
these peasants and fishermen, turning over in
their minds whether they can bring themselves
to this, and wondering why it should be expected
of them, he goes on to say : " For if ye forgive men
their trespasses, your heavenly Father will also
forgive you." His hearers nod approvingly, for
now they know that their self-denial will, in the
fulness of time, bring its own reward.

He asks even more. To love those who love
you—any heathen can do as much ! " Love your
enemies, bless them that curse you, do good to
them that hate you, and pray for them which
despitefully use you and persecute you." Love
one's enemy, that is a tough job ! One asks him :
" How oft shall my brother sin against me, and
I forgive him ? Till seven times ?" Jesus looks
squarely at the questioner, and answers forthwith :
" I say not unto thee, until seven times ; but, until
seventy times seven."

They are dumbfounded. They fancy that he
is going too far in this matter, as in many more.
Nevertheless, they understand his drift better
when he explains his seeming extravagance by
gently exhorting them : " Judge not, that ye be
not judged. For with what judgment ye judge,
ye shall be judged ; and with what measure ye
mete, it shall be measured to you again. . . .

Therefore all things whatsoever ye would that men should do to you, do ye even so to them : for this is the law and the prophets."

They do not know that, fifty years earlier, Hillel, the famous rabbi, had taught the same thing in very nearly the same words; all they know is that, to begin with, Hillel had been a poor working man, even as they are themselves. But they can see with their own eyes that Jesus does not sit in the Great Council at Jerusalem, does not dwell in the houses of the mighty, nor eat at the groaning tables of the rich. He comes to seek them out, the poor in their huts by the lakeside, far from temples and palaces. If he enjoys a glass of good wine, before he drinks it he has bent low to enter the cottage door, has looked at the baby in the cradle and asked how the live stock are faring, has played with the youngsters and brought the sick mother back to health. That is why they believe him when, seated at their frugal board, he says : " Blessed be ye poor, for yours is the kingdom of God. . . . Lay not up for yourselves treasures upon earth, where moth and rust doth corrupt, and where thieves break through and steal. But lay up for yourselves treasures in heaven ; for where your treasure is, there will your heart be also." Once more they nod approvingly. Robbers abound in Galilee. This man knows what he is talking about. They feel sure, therefore, that he must be equally well

informed when he promises them good things in
the kingdom of heaven.

Does he not follow his own rede ? " When thou
makest a dinner or a supper, call not thy friends,
nor thy brethren, neither thy kinsmen, nor thy
rich neighbours ; lest they also bid thee again,
and a recompense be made thee. But when thou
makest a feast, call the poor, the maimed, the
lame, the blind. And thou shalt be blessed, for
they cannot recompense thee. Thou shalt be
recompensed at the resurrection of the just."

Rich men are uneasy when they hear of this
teaching. A new disturber of the peace ; a man
who utters dangerous words to the common
people ! But some of the younger among them,
who have recently entered into their heritage, take
the message to heart. A wealthy youth comes
to him and asks : " What shall I do, that I may
inherit eternal life ? . . . The commandments ?
I have kept them all since my childhood's days.
What lack I yet ?" His aspirations and his
humility please the master, who would gladly
win him over. " Only one thing dost thou lack.
Go thy way, sell whatsoever thou hast, and give
to the poor ; so shalt thou have treasure in
heaven." This was too hard a saying for the
young man of great possessions. After looking
at Jesus for a moment, and wondering whether
the giver of such counsel could be in his right
mind, he went away sorrowful. Jesus watched

him go, and then, looking round, said : " How hardly shall they that have riches enter into the kingdom of God ! It is easier for a camel to go through the eye of a needle, than for a rich man to enter into the kingdom of heaven."

His followers have noticed that he is invariably gentle in his dealings with the well-to-do, although he regards the ownership of wealth as sinful. He is gentle to all sinners, and would almost seem to love them more than the righteous. How puzzling a contradiction ! Seeing the doubt in their faces, he bethinks himself of another parable that will make a special appeal to his present auditors— for the way in which he clothes his thoughts when speaking to them is determined by the promptings of the moment. " What man of you, having a hundred sheep, if he lose one of them, doth not leave the ninety and nine in the pasture, and go after that which is lost, until he find it ? And when he hath found it, he layeth it on his shoulders, rejoicing. And when he cometh home, he calleth together his friends and neigh- bours, saying unto them : ' Rejoice with me ; for I have found my sheep which was lost.' I say unto you, that likewise joy shall be in heaven over one sinner that repenteth, more than over ninety and nine just persons, which need no repentance."

He goes on to tell them the tale of a son who wasted his substance with riotous living, and at

last, penitent, returned to his father's house.
Thereupon the father kissed him, dressed him in
fine raiment, and had the fatted calf killed to
make a feast for him. The other son waxed
angry with the father, saying he had served for
many years, and kept all his father's commandments, but never had the father given him so
much as a kid, that he might make merry with
his friends. The father made answer : " Son,
thou art ever with me, and all that I have is thine.
It was meet that we should make merry, and
be glad : for this thy brother was dead, and is
alive again ; was lost, and is found."

What ? Had not the industrious son a good
right to be angry, when his father had not given
him so much as a kid in return for years of
faithful service ? Would the stream of human
love flow thus unjustly, were all the dams broken
down so that it could flow as freely as the river
of God's grace ? Then what counts is, not what
people actually do or leave undone, but what they
are feeling and thinking the while ? There is
an all-seeing eye which pierces the veil of semblance, to reach the human heart that beats
within, and to discern our hidden weaknesses !
Jesus embodies in his present teaching what he
learned in boyhood from his observation of the
strait-laced. Only where secret sins are concerned is he more rigorous than the law.

He knows that people are most inclined to make

solemn asseverations about matters as to which
they are not sure of themselves. Why should
a man swear by heaven ? Why should he swear
by his own head ? " Thou canst not make one
hair white or black. Let your conversation be,
Yea, yea, Nay, nay : for whatsoever is more than
these cometh of evil." Why, when a man gives
alms to the poor, should he have a trumpet
sounded before him, " as the hypocrites do in the
synagogues and in the streets, that they may have
glory of men ? Verily I say unto you, they have
their reward. But when thou doest alms, let not
thy left hand know what thy right hand doeth :
that thine alms may be in secret : and thy Father
who seeth in secret himself shall reward thee
openly." Why pray in public places, to be seen
of men ? " Enter into thy private room, and
when thou hast shut the door, pray to thy Father
who is in secret." Why, when fasting, pull a long
face, looking sallow and wan, that all may know
what thou art doing ? " When thou fastest,
anoint thy head and wash thy face."

Do not fancy that sacrifices will atone for
everything. " If thou bring thy gift to the altar,
and there rememberest that thy brother hath
aught against thee ; leave there thy gift before
the altar, and go thy way ; first be reconciled to
thy brother, and then come and offer thy gift."
Nay more, he, who has never known woman,
knows very well how to interpret the glances

that pass between the sexes on festal occasions.
This lust of the flesh, which he has not himself
experienced, was plain enough to him one day
at synagogue in the eyes of another man whom
he saw glancing covetously at a woman sitting
with the others apart. She made as if she did
not notice, and no breath of rumour betrayed the
infidelity of the pair—but Jesus read it in their
day-dream. That is why he now tells his hearers :
" Whosoever looketh on a woman to lust after
her, hath already committed adultery with her
in his heart."

Those to whom this shaft strikes home, lower
their eyelids abashed.

IV.

Yet there is nothing of the revivalist preacher
about him. The man who thus brings glad
tidings to the common people, never glorifies
poverty and sickness ; he is content to console
and to cure. He does not seek to cheer sinners
by promising them to take their sins upon his own
shoulders. " Sin no more !"—that is his message
to the saved. The keen enjoyment of life which
made the boy so full of gratitude towards the
Father, is redoubled in the grown man who can
now pour the treasures of his affection into so
many hearts. " Be not of a sad countenance
like the hypocrites," he cries to the pietists.

Illness is a sin, or a sign thereof ; and to one whom
he has cured he says : " Lo, thou art made whole :
sin no more, lest a worse thing come unto thee."
In perfect health, so fully master of his nerves
that he can sleep soundly on a boat in a raging
storm, frugal and temperate, happy in the conviction that he is God's child, he is free from
uneasiness as to what another day may bring,
and his favourite thoughts are of the animals and
plants that have been his familiar companions
since boyhood's days.

" Take no thought for your life, what ye shall
eat, or what ye shall drink ; nor yet for your
body, what ye shall put on. Is not the life more
than meat, and the body than raiment ? Behold
the birds of the air : they sow not, neither do
they reap nor gather into barns ; yet your
heavenly Father feedeth them. Are ye not much
better than they ? . . . Consider the lilies of the
field, how they grow ; they toil not, neither do
they spin. Yet I say unto you that even Solomon
in all his glory was not arrayed like one of these.
Wherefore, if God so clothe the grass of the field,
which to-day is, and to-morrow is cast into the
fire, shall he not much more clothe you, O ye
of little faith ? . . . Take therefore no thought
for the morrow : for the morrow shall take thought
for the things of itself."

He thankfully accepts whatever the day
chances to bring : whether it be a gathering in

the market place ; or a quiet talk with two or three of his disciples ; or an hour spent in solitary musing beside the waters of the lake ; or a cheerful banquet of lamb and white bread, washed down with red wine of the countryside. Once he is asked : " Why do the disciples of John fast, but thy disciples fast not ?" He answers, with a twinkle in his eye : " Can the children of the bridechamber fast, while the bridegroom is with them ? But the days will come, when the bridegroom shall be taken away from them, and then they shall fast in those days."

No rabbinical formulas are to damp their spirits when he and his followers sit down to a cheerful meal. It is needless to wash hands and table furniture in accordance with the pre-scriptions of an elaborate ritual. Why delay to utter a tedious succession of prayers, when a few well-chosen words, a suitable text from scripture, will suffice ? True, he does not seek to impose his ways on others. Let them offer up their sacrifices and say their prayers as they will. For his part, he does not offer up sacrifices ; he never baptises any one ; even the prayer of which he tells his disciples when one of them specially asks him how they should pray, does not become a formula, and is never mentioned again. A free spirit, he is bold enough to voice his glad tidings unconstrainedly, is satisfied to appeal to his hearers' hearts ; for in his view sin and grace are

inward matters, the fruit of the hidden workings
of unexpressed thoughts.

That is why he loves children, young folk, the
unlettered, the poor, whom no care for great
possessions can drive into crooked ways. When
certain women bring their children to him, and
his disciples are loath to admit them to his
presence, Jesus is much displeased, and says :
" Suffer the little children to come unto me, and
forbid them not : for of such is the kingdom of
heaven. Verily I say unto you, whosoever shall
not receive the kingdom of God as a little child,
he shall not enter in." Thereupon he takes the
children up in his arms, lays his hands upon them,
and blesses them.

In other ways, too, he finds it necessary to be
rather more severe with his disciples than comes
naturally to him. Like all the prophets before
him, and like John the Baptist, he needs this little
circle of faithful followers. With them, through
them, he can more speedily win the fame which
is essential to his influence. He chooses them in
accordance with his first impressions, and tells
them to follow him ; if any one offer himself
spontaneously, Jesus is distrustful, and repels the
advance. Yet, in the end, even those whom he
chose, forsook him.

Many of them have been disciples of the
Baptist. Some of them are the sons of well-to-do
people. All must put their possessions into the

common stock, upon which teacher and pupils live together, share and share alike. Those he loves best are: Simon, the practical; James, the inspired; and John, the tender-hearted. All three of them are pious, and yet selfish; unstable, and yet full of love. One day Jesus, walking on the shore of the lake, sees a customs officer, a member of a class regarded as infamous, sitting in his booth. Jesus does not hesitate. Wishing to set an example, he says "Follow me," and Levi, the publican, forsakes everything to heed the call. This man, known also as Matthew, is subsequently to do more than any one else to make the master's fame widely known. Another of those whom Jesus summons to his side is Simon the zealot, in earlier days a disciple of that Galilean rebel whose bold doings and tragical end had made so deep an impression on him in boyhood. All but one are Galileans. The exception is a man from the south of Judea, Judas Iscariot by name. No warning voice tells Jesus that it is unwise to admit among his intimates one whose chief associations are with the neighbourhood of Jerusalem.

As most of them are younger than himself, it is easy for him to guide them. He calls them his children and his labourers; bids them make ready the ship, row, provide victuals. When they do not understand him, he exclaims: " Know ye not this parable? How then will ye know all

parables ?"   But he does not found a community ;
he will not suffer them to give him any loftier
titles than " master " and " rabbi " ; and, in
a moment of exaltation, he tells them that they
are the salt of the earth and the light of the world.

He never loses patience with the women who
follow him in his wanderings.   Three or four stay
with him throughout ; new-made friends, for not
one of them is of his own kin, or a neighbour from
Nazareth.   They are wealthier folk than the men,
Joanna being actually the wife of Herod's steward.
She and Susanna have faith in him because he has
cured their infirmities.   Two other women go
with him because their sons have become his
disciples.

Since the essence of Jesus' teaching is love,
the women understand his words better than the
men ; and as he goes to and fro they cherish him
with a fervour which seems to him at once
unsuitable and suitable, which he does not ask
for and would none the less miss if it were lacking—for the very reason that he renounces a
close intimacy with womankind.   When they
anoint him, or sit at his feet listening, he fulfils
his heart's dreams of love, dividing as a prophet
among many women what the ordinary citizen
concentrates upon one.   Only because he feels
himself to be a man elect, only as an expression
of self-sufficiency, does he decry marriage, in
which husband and wife seek to please one

another, instead of trying to serve God. In practical life he does not insist upon chastity and celibacy, even in the case of his immediate followers. Two among those whom he chooses as disciples are married men. Peter can bring his wife as a member of the company. God joins men and women together; and Jesus, by forbidding divorce, seeks to protect marriage with a stronger buttress than that furnished by the Mosaic law. Accepting whatever devotion women choose to offer, he has a special fondness for those who show most enthusiasm in this regard. At the house where he is staying in a certain village there are two sisters. One of them, Martha, is overburdened with house work, while the other, Mary, comes to sit at Jesus' feet. When Martha asks him to bid Mary help in the chores, he smiles, and answers: "Martha, Martha, thou hast much to care for and art troubled with many occupations; but Mary hath chosen that good part, which shall not be taken away from her."

They all look upon the new teacher as a prophet, and he deems himself one. He does not make a higher claim than this, and sometimes claims even less. Nowhere does he ascribe to himself superhuman memories or hopes; never, at this period, does he even hint at an assumption of the Messianic role. When people say that he must be one of the old prophets come again, he

keeps his pleasure to himself, being prompt to turn their thoughts towards the kingdom of heaven and the Father of us all. If he is the son of the living God, it is in the sense in which all are this who feel in themselves the working of the creative force out of which we derive our being. Now he finds a new phrase, the better to express his lowliness, speaking of himself as the Son of Man. When the prophets of old had wished to draw attention to the vastness of the gulf which separated them from God, they were wont to describe themselves thus. Ezekiel repeatedly makes the Spirit of the Lord address him as " Son of Man "—a mortal in his weakness, born to suffer and to die, and yet equipped with all the dignity vouchsafed him by God's grace.

Jesus chose this appellation for himself out of Holy Writ, because he wanted the humblest name that the prophets had conceived. The Son of Man, he said, had come, not to be served, but to serve. Of his human coming and going he speaks in the terms that John had used before him ; and when the young man with great possessions addresses him as " Good Master," he refuses to accept the name, and chides the speaker with proud humility : " Why callest thou me good ? There is none good but one, that is God."

V.

Thus he leads a life out of touch with the main interests of his day and his nation.   Nevertheless, like any other Jew, he shuns contact with the heathen, who are regarded as impure ; he warns his disciples against them, and cannot bring himself to exert his powers of healing for their benefit.   He can speak of them only with abhorrence ; and when he is characterising a fault he says : " Do not as the heathen do."   The heathen seek after money and possessions ; the disciples must not carry the glad tidings to them, must not give that which is holy unto the dogs, nor cast pearls before swine.   They are to keep away from Samaria, the land with a mixed population, thrust in between the Jewish regions of Galilee and Judea ; and if he himself shuns Jerusalem, still more unwilling is he to carry to the Samaritans the message of the God whom the Jews worship in the temple.

Nor do his references to worldly affairs please most of his hearers.   He does not preach against Herod, though the tetrarch is keeping John the Baptist in prison ; he does not rail against Rome and its worldwide empire ; he does not censure the mighty.   When one of the company says, " Master, speak to my brother, that he divide the inheritance with me," he is angry, and replies : "Man, who made me a judge or a divider over you?" As an innovator he is cautious, always trying to link the new on to the old. "Think not that I am come to destroy the law, or the prophets : I am not come to destroy, but to fulfil. For verily I say unto you, till heaven and earth pass, one jot or one tittle shall in no wise pass from the law, till all be fulfilled."

He even tells the multitude to be guided by the Pharisees, to act as the law directs : "Go show yourselves to the priests. . . . What they say unto you, that do."

Nevertheless he is the enemy of these same priests, and they are his enemies.

Attentively they mark his first steps. They invite the new teacher to sit at board with them. The rulers of the synagogue in Capernaum argue with him, address him as "Rabbi," and listen to his guarded suppositions. But this phase is soon over. Their uneasiness grows as Jesus' fame spreads ; and they seek occasion to set the people against him. They find him at table, cheerful as ever, a guest among publicans and sinners, for Levi the customs officer has bidden friends to meet him. One of the Pharisees asks the disciples : "Why eateth your master with publicans and sinners?" Jesus, who is at the other end of the room, hearing the words or grasping the import of the question, fires up, and volleys at the enquirer (a man of unblemished reputation, but Jesus' deadly enemy) the fierce answer : " They that be whole need not a physician, but they that are sick. Go you and learn what that meaneth ; for I am not come to call the righteous, but sinners to repentance."

This is the first blow he directs against his enemies, the first delivered in all men's sight. He glares at the strangers, who depart in silence. The struggle has begun.

How are they to get the better of him ? One day he sits at meat with sinners—and the next, in the house of God, the congregation clamours for a sermon from him. They can do nothing against such popularity. The most dangerous innovators have always been fellows of his sort, men who begin to preach in the outlying dis- tricts, and do not belong to any brotherhood which can call them to account ; men who go into the villages and talk to the common people. Has he not railed against the wealthy, as if to have riches were a sin ? John the Baptist began his mission like that ; and John might by now have become a dangerous force, had not Herod put him under lock and key. Well, well, they must keep a wary eye on Jesus, but let him go his own way for the nonce. The more rope he has, the more his tongue has free play, the more speedily and surely will come the day when he will run his head against the civil law, and then we shall have him at a disadvantage.

One Sabbath day, Jesus and his disciples go
for a walk through the corn fields. May has
come, the grain is ripe, the young men are
hungry. They pluck the ears of corn, and eat.
Two Pharisees, spies who watch the doings of
this godless band, encounter them as if by chance,
and ask them why they are doing that which it
is not lawful to do on the Sabbath. For to the
Jews the Sabbath is specially sacred among
sacred things. Their superstition would even,
if it could, bind nature in chains ; and they speak
of intermittent springs as " sabbatical." Jesus,
whose way it is to talk to the folk in the vernacular, but to answer the scribes and Pharisees
in the words of Holy Writ, says : " Have ye never
read what David did, when he had need and was
an hungered, he and they that were with him ?
How he went into the house of God, and did eat
the shewbread, which it is not lawful for any
but the priests to eat, and gave also to them that
were with him ? . . . The Sabbath was made
for man, and not man for the Sabbath : therefore the Son of Man is Lord also of the Sabbath."
The two spies look at one another with horror.
He has desecrated the Sabbath !

A little while after this, persons come to him,
four of them carrying a man sick of the palsy.
Since there is such a press of people that they
cannot get near to the master, from the slope
against which the house where he is staying is

built, they climb on to the low, flat roof, and let down the stretcher into the inner court. Jesus, to whom illness is sin, says to the sick man : " Son, thy sins be forgiven thee." Certain of the scribes are present, and their thoughts run : " What blasphemy ! Who but God can forgive men's sins ?" Jesus divines their hostility, for even in a crowd he is prompt to recognise his foes, and he wrathfully answers the unspoken words : " What reason ye in your hearts ? Is it easier to say, ' Thy sins are forgiven thee'; or to say, ' Rise up and walk ' ?" Under stress of the speaker's magnetic power, the sick man thereupon rises to his feet, picks up the pallet on which he has been lying, and walks away.

The onlookers are more than a little frightened ; they dare not acclaim the master for what he has done ; it is they who are now as if palsied. They glorify God, and say one to another : " We have seen strange things to-day !" But the Pharisees when they get home and are behind closed doors, raise hands in reprobation. He has blasphemed God ! He has forgiven sins ! He is worthy of death !

But they do not dare to say such words aloud, for the common folk love Jesus ; and here in restless Galilee, far from the great capital, it is a risky matter to lay hold of a leader of the people. They go to and fro, therefore, saying that the new rabbi lures women away from domestic duties. But Jesus, stirred and enheartened, begins, for his part, to utter his thoughts without reserve. He relates in a parable how two men went up into the temple to pray ; the one a Pharisee, and the other a publican. The Pharisee stood and prayed thus within himself : " God, I thank thee that I am not as other men are, extortioners, unjust, adulterers, or even as this publican. I fast twice in the week, I give tithes of all that I possess." And the publican, standing afar off, would not lift up so much as his eyes to heaven, but smote upon his breast, saying: " God be merciful to me a sinner." Jesus' auditors are wondering how he will end his parable. Will he venture to speak well of the sinner ? Yes, he does so ! "I tell you, this man went down to his house justified, rather than the other: for every one that exalteth himself shall be abased ; and he that humbleth himself shall be exalted."

All Galilee knew, ere long, that Jesus of Nazareth was an enemy of the scribes and the Pharisees. Soon the Sanhedrim, the Great Council in Jerusalem, knew it too ; for its members, through their agents, kept careful watch upon the sayings and doings of innovators in God's State. " Follow him up ! Put temptation in his way !" came the word from Jerusalem. Again, therefore, one of the Pharisees invited him to dinner ; and he went into the

Pharisee's house, and sat down to meat. While they were at table, the door opened and a woman, young and pretty, whom every one knew to be a harlot, came in. She had heard of the kindly rabbi, who loved sinners. How could she get near him ? If she tried to reach him when he was amid the multitude, they laughed at her, and would not let her pass. She had been waiting for the chance of finding him in a house where few people were ; and, debating within herself what she could bring to please him, she could think of nothing but the fragrant oil with which it was her wont to anoint her body that it might be more pleasing to those who purchased her love.

Now she sees him at the board. The gentleness of his countenance, contrasting so strongly with the harsh faces of the others, is too much for her composure, and she falls at his feet weeping. She washes his feet with her tears, and looks round for a cloth to wipe them. All stare at her, dumb with amazement, and no one offers to help her in her search ; so in the end she uses, instead of a cloth, the long hair which is one of her charms. Having wiped his feet with her hair, she kisses them passionately, still sobbing ; and, with trembling hands, she proceeds to anoint them with the contents of her phial. All the while she keeps her eyes lowered, not daring to raise them to Jesus' face.

The host is angered. He thinks : "This man, if he were a prophet, would have known who and what manner of woman she is that toucheth him ; for she is a harlot."

Jesus reads the thought, and answers them aloud.

"Simon, I have somewhat to say unto thee."

"Master, say on."

"There was a certain creditor who had two debtors : the one owed five hundred pence, and the other fifty. And when they had nothing to pay, he freely forgave them both. Tell me, therefore, which of them will love him most."

"I suppose," answers Simon, "the debtor to whom he forgave most."

"Thou hast rightly judged," says Jesus, in a grave and quiet tone.

Then, after glancing down upon the woman at his feet, he turns back to Simon, and goes on :

"Seest thou this woman ? I entered into thy house, thou gavest me no water for my feet ; but she hath washed my feet with tears, and wiped them with the hairs of her head. Thou gavest me no kiss : but this woman, since the time I came in, hath not ceased to kiss my feet. My head with oil thou didst not anoint : but this woman hath anointed my feet. Wherefore I say unto thee, her sins, which are many, are forgiven ; for she loved much : but to whom little is forgiven, the same loveth little."

His hearers are so much horrified at these blasphemous utterances, that they cannot say a word in reply. Amid the silence, the pair would almost seem to be alone in the room : the prophet and the sinner, linked by the woman's caressive touch, by her kissing of the feet she has watered with her tears and dried with her hair ; wedded for a moment by the man's loving words : a woman who has sold herself to all comers ; a man who has never known woman. A new word, which is to ring down the ages, has been spoken in the house of a small trader, by the shores of a remote lake, far from the busy life of the world ; and the auditors in the little room are so much alarmed that they can only sit mumchance.

Then the man helps the woman to her feet, and says gently : " Thy sins are forgiven. Thy faith has saved thee. Go in peace."

She went away, to return and follow his foot-steps. She had come to him from Magdala, under stress of new and obscure longings. When this stranger had spoken to her so tenderly, she had wept bitter tears. Who, ere this, had spoken to her tenderly unless when moved by a fleeting desire for carnal possession ? But he had raised her from her abasement, a physician ministering to her distress. Following him throughout the time of his mission, she was keen-witted enough to discern what no other among his followers could see, his power of renunciation. She was better able to understand him than were any of his disciples, for the very reason that her life before she knew him had been the sport of blind lusts.

That was why, when all the disciples had fled, Mary of Magdala stood beneath the cross, and was the first to make Jesus immortal by her dream of his resurrection.

VI.

John was in prison. When he went to the grating through which his meals were passed and through which as much fresh air as reached him filtered into his cell, all he could see was part of the outer wall of the fortress where he was confined, a sheer wall built of huge blocks of black basalt. Pressing his face to the bars, he could even catch a glimpse of the white limestone rock from which the wall sprang. Sometimes mist rising from the valley made the damp abiding-place even damper. The soldiers who moved to and fro in the outer yard, and glanced from time to time at the caged Baptist—now mockingly and now with compassion—were strangers to him, and spoke a tongue he could not understand, for they were Moabites or Idumæans.

What is he thinking of? Images from the days

beside Jordan course through his mind. Then his thoughts roam back to his life as an anchorite in the wilderness. Less vivid are the memories of his childhood in the great city. Now, for the hundredth time, he rereads the writings of the prophets Daniel and Isaiah. These men are his models. He tries to guide himself by the story of their struggles. Does he still believe that freedom will come ; in the end, a victory ? Or will his fate be like that of Moses, who from the top of Mount Nebo (hard by the fortress) caught his last glimpse of the promised land. Moses, too, had been full of wrath at the people's lack of faith. Does John himself now believe in their steadfastness ? From week to week, he numbers the days to the expected return of some of the most faithful of his disciples, whom he has sent to gather news—for he is allowed to talk to them through the grating. They are the doves he has sent forth to learn the state of the great flood which began by Jordan ; the flood whose waters, he hopes, will continue to rise.

The last time they came back, they had had much to say about a man from Nazareth, whose name was in every one's mouth. One of those, it would seem, whom John himself had baptised ; but his efforts to recall this particular face from among hundreds upon hundreds were of no avail. Galilee, said the messengers, was ringing with Jesus' fame, was buzzing with talk of his wonder-

ful deeds. Strange deeds, thought John ; unholy
things. Orgies with publicans and harlots. The
new teacher and his disciples did not fast, and
Jesus was said to be often in merry mood. Glad
tidings ? Why glad ? Why did he not make
people confess, and then baptise them ? Still,
what Jesus was said to teach about the kingdom
of heaven ; his denunciations of the rich and the
mighty ; his preaching to vast multitudes that
flocked to hear him, multitudes that no synagogue
could hold—these things did not seem amiss
to the captive. How strange it was that this
Jesus should have cropped up the moment after
he himself had been cast into prison ? Was it
not to be expected that the people would regard
the man of Nazareth as the Baptist's successor ?
John remembered his own words : " He that
cometh after me is mightier than I." That
saying must have smoothed the newcomer's
path. What if the Nazarene, who was now
reaping advantage from John's work as forerunner, were but a false prophet and a charlatan ?

The cell-door rattles ; it grates on its hinges ;
it opens. Two soldiers enter, and sign to him
to follow them. Is he to go to his death ? Tense
with expectation and alarm, he passes out of the
crypt with his gaolers. They lead him, not to a
dark courtyard, but up the great stairway, to
the palace of the tetrarch.

Herod Antipas was a weakling, a man of

timid disposition, the slave of his lusts; and he lacked his father's malevolent energy. When he was visiting Rome as the guest of his brother, this brother's wife, Herodias, divined in Herod Antipas a stepping-stone to power, for her then husband, a nerveless creature, was nothing but a satellite of the emperor. Herodias, a grand-daughter of Herod the Great, had in her more of that monarch's toughness of fibre, and the strength that enables people to carry out what they plan. Soon she was able to lead her brother-in-law astray, fascinating him by her beauty, inducing him to put away his first wife that he might take his new love back with him as consort. The divorced princess, daughter of Aretas, an Arabian king, had fled to this fortress of Machærus, one of her father's strongholds. There had been a war, in the course of which Herod had got possession of the place. Since then, he had spent much of his time at Machærus, on the frontier of Araby, for it was easier to keep the borderland quiet from such a vantage ground than from the comparatively remote Tiberias in Galilee.

The gloomy fanatic, John, was in his right place here, in the desolate land eastward of the Dead Sea, with its precipitous valleys, its sulphur springs, and its volcanic rocks. Hither had the tetrarch's soldiers brought him in the spring, when the masses swarming round him on Jordan's

bank began to be numbered by thousands, and
the authorities in Jerusalem were dreading a
new revolt. Pilate had doubtless taken counsel
with the Sanhedrim as to the measures that
would be most expedient. The gathering of
malcontents was beyond the borders of the land
directly under Roman rule, and the governor
had given the tributary prince a hint, saying that
Herod would do well to keep order in his own
country. Such troubles were perennial in this
part of the world, and must be nipped in the bud.
At the very time of the Baptist's arrest, some
sectaries had been assembling in the mountains
of Samaria, which was under Pilate's immediate
governance. Fearing that a revolt might be
imminent, he had sent legionaries to scatter
the possible disturbers of the place, to take
captive and to slay.

John is led through long arcades, past baths
paved with motley-coloured stones. From these
upper levels he can look down upon the water
tanks of the city, the war machines, and the
arsenal, all lying at the foot of the fortress. He has
been this way twice before.

He has been here before, as well; in the great
hall he now enters. Those who sit in the seats
of the mighty know how to hang sheets of brown
canvas, to keep their habitations cool during the
summer heats; and at a nod their slaves hasten
to bring them iced fruits for refreshment. A man

needs all the fortitude of a revivalist preacher if he is not to show weakness when within a minute or two he is brought, as John has been brought, from a dark and stifling dungeon to these splendid apartments. True, the tetrarch, well on in years, reclining on cushions in the coolest corner of the room (handsome in youth he had been, but is now worn and jaded), does not seem to be one who would gladly torment his fellow human beings. But the woman behind the curtain— John sees it moving, and guesses that Herodias, who withdrew as he was brought in, is there listening to every word—is of another mould ; and though her charms are now over-ripe, she is still vigorous, and she knows how to bend her husband to her will.

From where he lies among the many-hued silks, the tetrarch looks up at the haggard visage of the prophet, who stands before him in rags. He is at once curious, alarmed, and amazed ; but would, if he could, hide these feelings behind a mask of impassive weariness. John knows his thoughts, and is unaffrighted. The tenor of their conservation has not come down to us, except for this much. We know that the Baptist rebuked Herod for his marriage with Herodias and urged him to divorce her. Not only did the Jewish law forbid such a union with the wife of a living brother, not only had a twofold adultery thus been committed ; but in this case, further, there had been a hideous advantage taken of a brother's hospitality. The reproof was a familiar one in the house of Herod. Antipas' father, Herod the Great, had been censured by the priests of Jerusalem because of his many divorces and remarriages. But now the man who uttered the reproof was a poor prisoner, in a lonely fortress, where, at the ruler's whim, the headsman's axe would fall.

Yet the prisoner said his say, and the ruler hesitated to give the sign of doom. Why this hesitation? John's followers had dispersed, and a new prophet had arisen in his place; the guardians of the law were equally hostile to the Baptist and to his successor. Timid though the tetrarch was, what could hinder him, after such brazen defiance, after such an insult to his wife, from ordering the offender's instant execution? The fanatic stood before him, tall and lean, hairy and half naked, uttering harsh denunciations, voicing threats of eternal damnation. As soon as the Baptist had been taken back to his cell, Herodias would return, and would angrily accuse Herod of cowardice. Nevertheless, John's mien was so impressive, that the tetrarch was overawed. The captive was sent away scatheless to the crypt; free to receive tidings from his disciples; and free, therefore, to send messages forth into the land.

Nor is it long before the Baptist's disciples come

again to the prison, and tell their master of the
new successes of the man of Nazareth. Jesus has
now openly denounced the Pharisees, and they
have openly denounced him. Since he heals the
sick wherever he goes, contention spreads in
widening circles. Again John feels that Jesus
is carrying on his own work, is fighting as he
himself has fought. He does his utmost to over-
come his prejudices against the prophet who
makes merry and sits at board with all and sundry.
Once more he plies his disciples with questions
concerning the details of Jesus' preaching and
behaviour. Since he cannot again see Jesus
face to face, and since his thoughts are continually
reverting to the problem of his own mission and
its upshot, to the problem whether that mission
is to be fruitless after all, he decides to question
Jesus through another's mouth.

Even so, John is tormented by conflicting
hopes and fears. If Jesus acknowledges himself
to be the long-expected Messiah, the Baptist's
sufferings will be atoned for, his work will not have
been wasted, his life will have a meaning. On
the other hand, even though Jesus be the one
greater than himself whose coming John has
foreseen, John cannot bring himself to approve
methods which contrast so strangely with those
of the prophets of earlier days. The enquiry
which he therefore entrusts to his disciples
embodies all the weariness and unending

impatience of the man behind prison bars : " Art thou he that should come, or do we look for another ?"

VII.

Jesus had never spoken of the Baptist. It seemed as if the memories of his encounter with John had been thrust out of his mind. Coupled with memories of John were those of the most terrible moment of his life, when he had come up out of the waters of Jordan ; had, with the eyes of inner vision, seen the dove descending ; and suddenly, as if from a great distance, had heard his Father's voice. Had that been only last spring ? Had it been but a few months ago when he had come back from the wilderness in a state of mental confusion, and when the first persons he had met had told him how John had been seized and taken to prison ?

Though he said no word of John, who was a prophet of his own time, he had much to say of the earlier prophets ; for in all he did he aimed at preserving the old, while refashioning it. Nothing could be more uncongenial to him than the destructive zealotry of Judas the Galilean, whose life and death had cast a gloom over his youth. He refers to Isaiah's condemnation of the self-righteous ; and he reiterates Hosea's demand for mercy rather than sacrifice. He follows in the footsteps of the prophets, the great tribunes of the people, the men who, hundreds of years before himself, had classed the rich among the ungodly—the better to extol the poor. He finds a man after his own heart in the writer of the Book of Enoch. This prophet, too, had been a Son of Man ; had declared that kings would be shorn of their glories, and cast into hell ; had exclaimed : "Woe unto you who build your palaces with others' sweat ! Every stone is a crime !"

The summer had passed its prime ; and when the shrivelling of the vine-leaves began, when the harvest of grain and of olives had been garnered, the honeymoon season of Jesus' career (that career on which he had been launched by his encounter with John) seemed likewise on the wane. True, people still flocked to him in increasing numbers. He had traversed all the towns and villages lying near the west of the Sea of Galilee, and had even crossed the lake to make his way into some of the valleys on its eastern shore and on the left bank of Jordan. But the field of his mission remained a small one, far from Judea, and therefore far from the area where Rome held sway ; always in the tetrarchy, and without attracting much attention from the authorities. Of course, these knew well enough what was afoot ; but they were tolerant, not regarding the fanaticism of poor peasants, fishermen, and artisans as of serious moment.

Nevertheless, the sick folk had become a weariness to Jesus. He seemed to feel ashamed of his talent for healing by suggestion, and to fear that its exercise was overshadowing his work as a teacher. People were already saying of him that he was possessed ; and beyond question he believed that there was a wrestle between his own spirit and a hostile spirit when he drove a devil out of another's body. He was growing tired. On one occasion a sick woman hoping for a cure came up behind him in the press and touched his garment ; thereupon Jesus felt that strength had gone out of him. At other times, illness reclaimed its victim after he had gone away. In his cheerful progress, through the cornfields, by the lake shore, how often do the possessed, the blind, the palsy-stricken call piteously after him ! They bar his route ; interrupt his preaching ; dim the joy of his life. When he fails to cure them (because of their own lack of faith), they regard him with terror, for they fancy that he has consigned them to the tortures of the damned. Can we be surprised that when he bids farewell to those whom he has restored to health, it is not with a gentle glance and a kindly word, but always with an urgent, almost threatening, injunction to silence?

One day he is in a crowded market place, where

he is perforce playing his customary part of healer and preacher rolled into one, when John's two messengers arrive. They are amazed at the size of the gathering. Perhaps, as they see Jesus sitting at ease in the open, their hearts are stirred with a sense of injustice, and they may even feel reproachful, for their own master is languishing in a noisome jail. It may be that Jesus guesses their thoughts, sympathises with the feelings aroused in their minds by the contrast. He looks at them searchingly, and asks : " What would ye know?" In John's name they answer : " Art thou he that should come, or do we look for another ?"

Jesus feels as if he were being touched by unfamiliar, intrusive hands. A momentous, a divine problem ; a question which no one can venture to ask himself, and which still less, therefore, John should dare to ask ; secrets between Father and Son, ineffable things, as tenuous as the golden-red cloud wreaths of the sunset sky, as ethereal as nocturnal musings ; the Son of Man's most intimate communings, and his shy reluctance to avow himself—all this is now dragged forth into the public square by a stranger, in a crude enquiry, which he is to answer point-blank with a Yes or a No ! What has moved the prisoner, the gloomy prophet, to ask such a question of a man of kindlier mould, a free man ? What answer does John look for?

As Jesus ponders these questions, and debates within himself what answer he shall give, the inner voice begins to speak clearly once again. May not this message from the Baptist be a new sign? Does it not convey a message from the Father, an injunction to show more self-confidence? The first sign had come just after John had baptised him. The second sign had been the news of John's arrest. Perhaps this message from John is the third!

His thoughts are in a turmoil; his feelings are confused. He does not know whether minutes pass, or hours, while he is silent, and before he recovers his composure. When, at length, he speaks, his customary gentleness has vanished. Something of the spirit of the zealot whose message has troubled him, seems to have entered into him. Pride, too, the chilly pride with which he had faced his mother at Cana, suddenly masters him once more. As at Cana, so now, the carpenter has a kingly mien. With a wave of the arm, he points to the surrounding multitude, and says to the messengers: "Go and show John again those things which ye do hear and see. The blind receive their sight, and the lame walk; the lepers are cleansed, and the deaf hear; the dead are raised up, and the poor have the glad tidings preached to them. And blessed is he, whosoever shall not be offended in me!"

Does any one among the numberless onlookers

understand what has happened? The teacher, who has hitherto held aloof from the miracles he has wrought and the cures he has effected, who has never yet adduced them as proof of his worth, now lays the utmost stress on them when sending a message to a man who never cured the sick but put all his trust in the spoken word. At the close, Jesus even seems to threaten John, to imply that the Baptist's question has been dictated by irony and jealousy. Instead of sending consolation and greeting to the captive, he reprimands him in his prison !

But when the messengers have gone, Jesus, in whom the depths have been stirred by the question, the answer, and the searchings of heart that came between, for the first time begins to speak of John, of those who foretell the days that are to come, and of those that lack faith—whom heretofore he has treated leniently. His hearers are alarmed by the bitter phrases that stream from the mouth of the preacher who has been wont to utter friendly words : " What went ye out into the wilderness to see ? A reed shaken with the wind ? A man clothed in soft raiment ? Such are to be seen in kings' houses ! Or did ye wish to see a prophet ? He is more than a prophet, for of him was it written : ' Behold, I send my messenger before thy face, which shall prepare thy way before thee.' Verily I say unto you, among them that are born of woman there

hath not risen a greater than John the Baptist ;
notwithstanding he that is least in the kingdom
of heaven is greater than John. . . . This is
Elijah, who was to come. He that hath ears to
hear, let him hear."

All are amazed at his tone. But the few that
understand the drift of his words, stare at him,
struck dumb with alarm ; for if he thus names
John " Elijah," if he thus describes the Baptist
as the man who has prepared the way, it must be
with the implication that he himself is the
Messiah. He must mean this, though he does not
say it in so many words. Hearken to him as he
goes on :

" But whereunto shall I liken this generation ?
It is like unto children sitting in the markets,
and calling unto their fellows, and saying : ' We
have piped unto you, and ye have not danced ;
we have mourned unto you, and ye have not
lamented.' For John came, neither eating nor
drinking, and they say : ' He hath a devil !'
Then came the Son of Man, eating and drinking,
and they say : ' Behold a man gluttonous, and
a winebibber, a friend of publicans and sinners !' "

VIII.

What a path has suddenly opened before him,
menacing yet alluring ! John's question is full
of temptation ; yet perhaps it is a sign from the

Lord. All the self-feeling he has allowed to
slumber within him since childhood's days, to
slumber because he walked with God and not
with men ; all that heretofore has only surged up
in rare moments, as in the hour of his baptism
and in the hour when he heard the news of
John's arrest—the sluice-gates have been opened
for a mighty rush by the Baptist's enquiry. By
turns he shivers with dread and glows with pride.
He hesitates. But when he recalls that this is
now the third occasion on which something
connected with the Baptist has set all his pulses
throbbing, his reverence for the prophets makes
him feel all the more convinced that John must
indeed be the messenger sent to prepare the way.
In imagination he looks his enemies in the face
and wonders what they are plotting against him ;
he contemplates the multitude, an ever-growing
multitude, of the faithful, the cured, the wor-
shippers. He has dreamed of a high calling, but
has shunned it as a waking thought. Now the
call is louder and clearer, comes to him from close
at hand.

Signs of strong emotion were to be marked in
the prophet when this incident was over. Before
ending his discourse he had upbraided the cities
wherein most of his cures had been wrought,
because they repented not. The day would
come, and soon, when they would be requited
with a worse fate than that of Sodom. His

animus, his angry tone, the bitterness of his words,
are new, so that many shake their heads. But
Jesus, accompanied by only a few of his disciples,
withdraws into the valleys on the eastern shore of
the lake ; and he is more reserved than before.

He is still brooding over what has happened,
when his disciples tell him that his mother and his
brothers have set out to lay hold of him, saying :
" He is beside himself !" Up till now, in truth,
he has been inclined to pour cold water on the
flames of enthusiasm. Once, when a woman
in an ecstatic condition had called to him from
the crowd, " Blessed is the womb that bare thee,"
far from thanking her for what she had said, he
had rejoined, with the aloofness that had characterised him since his mission had cut him off
from the life of home, " Yea, rather, blessed
are they that hear the word of God, and
keep it."

But now he is wounded to the quick that, when
he is in sore spiritual tribulation, they should
look upon him as one possessed. When his heart
is already racked, how can such a misunderstand-
ing fail to push him along the road leading
towards morbid exaltation ? It spurs him on to
put matters to a test among his own folk, since,
while all the rest of Galilee esteems him, they
alone regard him as an errant son and a madman.
His native village is not far away. If he makes
an early start, he can get there soon after

nightfall. He tells his disciples to stay where
they are, for he wishes to go alone. Skirting the
southern shore of the Sea of Galilee, he walks
thence westward through the foothills, leaving
Mount Tabor on his left. Now he knows every
step of the way.

Was it really no more than a few months since
he had joined the wedding feast at Cana, had
made wine for the guests there, and fashioned
certainty for himself? A few short months in
which he had wandered through a whole world
in the inner man! But there are the lights of
the little white town, peacefully cradled in
the mountain valley, just as of old, lulled by
the murmur of running waters. He enters the
cottage door. How startled they are! It is
natural that Brother James should be rather
upset, for James is a pietist, a stickler for the
law, and a follower of the Pharisees. But Mother
Mary and his sisters, too, are by no means easy
at the sight of him ; this itinerant preacher
and wonder-worker, who had abandoned his
carpenter's bench without a word of warning,
and has now come back as quietly as he had
departed. There he stands, as if nothing had
happened in the meantime. To-morrow is the
Sabbath. What will he do then ?

Next morning, in the synagogue where he has
spent half his youth as a silent onlooker, he rises
and informs the rulers that he wishes to speak.

They cannot say him nay. The servitor brings
him the roll, the book of the prophet Isaiah. All
eyes are fastened upon this child of Nazareth.
The congregation regards him with mixed feelings of curiosity and distrust. What will be the
nature of his preaching. Will he touch their
hearts with gentle words, as he has so often
touched hearts elsewhere? Jesus unrolls the
parchment a little farther, finds the passage he
wants, and reads aloud : " The Spirit of the Lord
is upon me, because he hath anointed me to
preach the gospel to the poor ; he hath sent me
to heal the brokenhearted, to preach deliverance
to the captives, and recovering of sight to the
blind, to set at liberty them that are bruised, to
preach the acceptable year of the Lord." Now
he closes the roll and hands it back to the servitor,
goes up into the pulpit, and looks steadily at the
familiar faces. Then, after a pause, he says :
" To-day is this scripture fulfilled in your ears."
They are taken aback. What can his meaning
be? But he goes on speaking, though all his
words have not come down to us. The hearers
nod assent and murmur approval. Yet there are
doubters among them who say : " From whence
has this man these things ? . . . Is he not the
carpenter, the son of Mary, the brother of James,
Joses, Judas, and Simon? Are not his sisters
here with us ?" Incredulity spreads among
them.

Jesus, now a practised speaker, notes the first
signs of hostility, is challenged thereby, and
apostrophises his fellow townsmen thus : " Ye
will surely say unto me, 'Physician, heal thyself.
We have been told thou hast done mighty works
in Capernaum. Do them here likewise, in the
place where thou wast born.' " He addresses
them in this way because he thinks that the fame
of his doings will be helpful to his influence among
them. Yet there is worse trouble in store. He
goes on : " Verily I say unto you, no prophet is
accepted in his own country. But I tell you of
a truth, many widows were in Israel in the days
of Isaiah, when the heaven was shut up three
years and six months, so that there was a great
famine throughout all the land. But unto none
of them was Isaiah sent, save unto Sareta, a city
of Sison, unto a woman that was a heathen widow.
And there were many lepers in Israel in the time
of Elisha the prophet, and none of them were
cleansed, saving Naaman the heathen !"

The preacher has done for himself now ! The
whole congregation rises in its wrath. " He is
making a mock of us ; has chosen examples from
the heathen to teach us faith and show us the
path of salvation !—Did you hear what he
said ?—He must be beside himself, as his own
mother declares !—The adulation of the women
of the lake shore has turned his head, has swelled
him with pride, has filled him with impious

thoughts.—He comes back to his birthplace, and
blasphemes God !"

Standing there in the synagogue, he sees
threatening hands uplifted. Glancing round, he
recognises the self-righteous elder, the rich man
who, aforetime, was his special aversion. This
worthy is shouting denunciations more loudly
than all the rest. What Jesus has long foreseen,
is now coming to pass ; what was written, is now
to be fulfilled. He feels that he has been guided
into this struggle, that a long road of resplendent
suffering lies open before him. As he stands and
turns these things over in his mind, the wrathful
townsmen close in upon him. They seize him,
and thrust him forth from the house of God. A
raging mob, they hurry him to the brow of the
hill on which, in boyhood, he used to lie dreaming
of the Father. One side of it is a precipice, well
known to him of old. From this they design to
cast him down headlong.

But here he is at home, knows every nook and
cranny of the mountain side. This was where
he used to lie in boyhood dreaming of the Father.
It is his Father's sacred pasture-land, and no one
can kill him here. While the infuriated crowd
is looking for the best place from which to make
an end of him, and while some of the cooler heads
are perhaps disputing with the rest as to whether
an execution without a trial may not get them all
into trouble, he slips from the hands that hold

him, is lost in the throng, and escapes to a haven
of refuge where he had sometimes hidden as
a child.

Saved from this imminent peril, he draws a
breath of relief. As he looks round from his
eyrie, his self-confidence is strengthened by the
thought of what has just taken place. He feels
that he has won his first battle. They scorned
him, and sought to kill him. God has saved him
from destruction. The old ties have been
severed now, the last vestiges of sentimental
attachment to early associations have disappeared.
Since those who should have been most ready
to accept him have despised him and rejected
him, neither family nor birthplace can any longer
have a meaning for him, and even the sense of
nationality fades away into nothingness. An
outcast, barely escaped from a violent death, his
one longing is for human sympathy.

When he gets back to his disciples, the decision
is for instant flight. Away from Galilee; that is
his one thought. A day later they have crossed
the Samaritan frontier, and are in the land of
the heathen. Here, at any rate, in the coasts
of Tyre and Sidon, no one will seek his life !
Still, even here, there are persons to whom his
face is known. He has not been long in Samaria
when a woman of Canaan recognises him. She
is in sore trouble, and wants his help, so she seeks
to flatter him by addressing him with a Jewish

title : " Have mercy on me, O Lord, thou son
of David ; my daughter is grievously vexed with
a devil." Jesus, whose practice it has been to help
none but Jews, answers not a word, but goes on
his way. Then his disciples intercede, begging
him to content her. " Send her away, for she
crieth after us !" None the less he clings to
the law, and to his own established usage. For
the second time he shakes his head, answering
them : " I am sent only to the lost sheep of the
house of Israel."

The woman is persistent. She overtakes him,
prostrates herself in front of him, and adjures
him : " Lord, help me !" A third time he
resists the promptings of his own heart, and
rejoins cruelly : " It is not meet to take the
children's bread, and to cast it to dogs." But a
mother's anxiety sharpens her wits, and she
makes the inspired answer : " True, Lord : yet
the dogs eat of the crumbs which fall from their
masters' table !"

These words snap the last threads that bind
him to the commandments learned in youth.
He feels that the woman of Canaan is no less
deserving of help than any Jewess, though she
be a heathen and an idolatress, wont to pray to
graven images. He is profoundly moved. Before him, kneeling in the dust, is the poor Canaan-
itess ; but, with the seer's vision, Jesus sees in
her the emblem of a new world, craving

deliverance. Casting to the winds the illusion that his own Jewish people is better than any other, he opens his heart to all mankind, regardless of dwelling-places and customs. He answers : " O woman, great is thy faith. Be it unto thee even as thou wilt !"

In this wise was for the first time a Gentile made whole by Jesus.

CHAPTER THREE

THE SHADOWS DARKEN

I.

Now begins the flight. During the summer, the prophet has been wandering through his native province, wishful only to comfort the afflicted and to make the sick whole. Never has he incited any to rebel against the ruler of the land, to raise their hands against the rich and the mighty. Never has he tried to harm the leaders of the theocracy in Jerusalem. But now, Jesus, the gentle, the serene, must spend the autumn and the winter (six months and more) as a fugitive, must hide in woods and in caves, must cross and recross the lake, and must even overstep the frontier, in order to escape his persecutors.

Ended is the festal season of journeyings through towns and villages, the joy of congenial activity, the happiness of effecting conversions. The limpid stream of love, flowing out to meet him from thousands upon thousands of hearts, has swelled to a mighty river, whose waters are yellow and turbid, for with them are mingled

undercurrents that mar the clarity of the whole.
Vanished is the sense of effortless victory, which
inspired him with humility in view of his Father's
grace. Gone is the simple innocence of his first
steps, before the chill wind of disfavour had begun
to blow athwart his path. This good man, the
herald of good tidings, has now to encounter
furtive adversaries; misconstruction, calumny,
and (deadliest of all) mockery. These foes
burden his spirit. They drive his self-confidence
from its secret recesses, till, multiplied a thousandfold, it becomes overweening. Consequently,
his intelligence is darkened; humility gives place
to an assumption of royal bearing; and the
Son of Man comes to regard himself as the
Son of God.

To begin with, it would seem, he fled by boat
to the land of Golan, and to Bethsaida, which
lies in the quiet, fertile alluvial country to the
north-east of the Sea of Galilee. Till recently
this region had been part of the tetrarchy of
Philip, the best among the sons of Herod the
Great. When he died, it had lapsed into the
hands of the overlord, Rome, and had been
incorporated into the province of Syria. But
Damascus, the new capital, was far away;
Rome, whence the orders came, was farther; and
Herod Antipas could not venture to interfere
with the happenings in the masterless neighbouring territory. The confusions attendant on

a period of transition made the place comparatively safe for such a fugitive as Jesus. We
do not know how long he stayed there in peace ;
this much is certain, that later in the year he
made his way southward into Decapolis, and
appeared at Gadara, a small Syrian town inhabited mainly by Greeks and lying to the
south-east of the lake. There, he thought, he
would be safe from his enemies ; no one would
surely dream of looking for a Jewish teacher in a
heathen stronghold.

His work as healer, however, drove him away
from this city of refuge. In the valley adjoining
the town, where, near the mountains, a great
herd of swine was feeding, there hastened to
meet him, forcing a way through the swineherds,
a man possessed. He had his dwelling among the
tombs and in caves, and none could tame him.
Often had he been bound with fetters and chains,
but the chains had been plucked asunder by
him, and the fetters broken in pieces. Always,
by day and by night, he was in the mountains
and in the tombs, shouting, and throwing stones
at all who came nigh. Now, having caught
sight of the prophet from afar, he ran up, crying
with a loud voice (like the possessed man in the
synagogue at Capernaum) : " What have I to
do with thee, Jesus, thou Son of the most high
God ?" Then, after the manner of a woman
who would fain be seduced, he went on : " I

adjure thee that thou torment me not!" Jesus said : "What is thy name?" In a flash came the answer : "My name is Legion, for we are many!" Jesus, facing him steadfastly, dominated him by word and by look, so that his frenzy was appeased, and, for the time at any rate, the demoniac grew sane. Meanwhile the swineherds, watching with tense interest, had neglected their charges, and at this moment some of the swine, which had strayed too near the cliff edge, fell headlong into the waters beneath.

The swineherds were terror-stricken, believing in their superstitious alarm that the devils, driven out of the possessed man, had entered into the dumb beasts. Fleeing into the city, they told the tale with manifold exaggerations, each embroidering the other's version. As a result, the townsmen came forth in a body to see how much truth there was in the story. They found that the demoniac had indeed been tamed, and that some of the swine had indeed been drowned. They found Jesus, at whose feet sat the sometime demoniac clothed and in his right mind ; Jesus who, beyond question, was answerable for all that had happened. They dreaded this sorcerer, and they besought him to depart out of their coasts, never to return.

A shadow had fallen upon his doings, so that people drove the benefactor away. Why? Was

it merely because a couple of swine had perished ?
Ere long, rumour would multiply two or three
into a thousand, even as the demoniac had
fancied himself possessed by a legion of devils.
It would seem as if, under stress of persecution,
he must have acquired characteristics which had
robbed him of much of his charm. One to whom
all doors had been freely opened, had become
one to avoid, one to drive away, now that he
had the hasty step, the questing glance, the dis-
cordant voice, of the hunted man. He had no
option but to return to Galilee, for his homeland
was his only refuge, though it was one where
danger still threatened from numerous enemies.

In Galilee were the Pharisees, on the prowl
for Jesus. Where, they wondered, had he hidden
himself away ? The story of his visit to Nazareth,
and of all that had taken place on that occasion,
had long since gone the round. No longer did
he show himself in the synagogues, gather
crowds to hear him preach on the hillside or
by the lake shore, sit at board openly with his
disciples. Was he, then, so greatly alarmed ;
and was that why he had kept out of sight for
so long ? Now, when he was back in Galilee
and could not remain hidden even for a day,
the news of his return spread swiftly from one
to another, and was known within forty-eight
hours throughout the towns and villages bordering the lake. But his adversaries did not raise

a public commotion, as the Nazarenes had done.
They walked warily, thinking it better to probe
him in conversation, and thus haply to discover
a weak spot before venturing upon open onslaught.

Yet it is enough for him to see them coming
to meet him, to recognise them by the primness
of their deportment, by the restraint of their
gestures, by their prying and penetrating gaze,
by their pursed lips, and by the frigid politeness
of their greeting—instantly an inner disquiet
warns him of the presence of his foes. Thereupon, all the currents of kindly feeling which
ordinarily flowed forth with such generous
abundance towards his fellow creatures, dry up
at the source. Two of the Pharisees, encounter-
ing him as if by chance, question him, with
an assumption of sincerity : " Master, when
shall the kingdom of God come ?" Jesus shows
no less restraint than those who seek to trap him,
and answers simply, like one who gives information without any hint of reproof : " The kingdom
of God cometh not with anxious watching, but
unawares. Neither shall they say ' Behold it is
there !' for the kingdom of God is within you."
With these words, which contain the essence
of his teaching, he goes on his way. The
Pharisees follow him with their eyes, and shrug
their shoulders. This prophetic message is beyond their understanding. A new thought, one
strong enough to shake the old world to its

foundations, has been uttered by the roadside as the carpenter passed on his way. But the two self-righteous hearers are deaf to the rustle of unseen wings. All they know is that he has said nothing they can complain of.

Another day, more of them come, determined to tempt the false prophet. " Show us a sign from heaven," they exclaim. Anger flames up in him, and he would gladly give his wrath free vent. But again he holds himself in check, and is content to answer bitingly : " A sign ? When it is evening, ye say : ' It will be fair weather, for the sky is red.' And in the morning : ' It will be foul weather to-day, for the sky is red and louring.' O ye hypocrites, ye can read the face of the sky ; but can ye not read the signs of the times ? Why doth this generation seek after a sign ? Verily I say unto you, there shall be no sign given unto you."

In truth the sky is red and louring ; the signs are there ; soon the storm will burst. The authorities in Jerusalem are growing weary of the succession of reports concerning the activities of the man of Nazareth. They have charged some of the scribes to visit Galilee and see how great is the prophet's following, to learn whether he blasphemes God, and to contrive the best means for laying him fast. The emissaries have no difficulty in finding him of whom they are in search, for once more there is a gathering of the people wherever he goes, and this crowd of witnesses is the very thing that his enemies desire.

Fruitlessly, at first, they walk round the outskirts of the throng, in the hope of hearing some tale of wickedness. The only reward for their zeal is the information that the disciples do not wash their hands before meals. Such ablutions are enjoined by the law, though only in the case of sacrificial repasts. According to a recent interpretation, however, they are also necessary as a prelude to ordinary meals, and the practice has become a fashion in the capital. Still, the poor peasants who dwell in these outlying districts have scarcely heard of the custom. It is a starting-point, nevertheless, from which this sedition-monger can, perhaps, be lured on to commit himself more seriously.—We may presume that it was in some market place, at eventide, when people were squatting in front of their houses or leaning against the door-posts, enjoying the cool of the hour before sunset, when the scholars from Jerusalem accosted the master, and put him the question point-blank : " Why do thy disciples transgress the tradition of the elders ? They wash not their hands when they eat bread."

The livelong day Jesus has marked these questioners. Even when they were not in sight he has felt their nearness. In them for the first

time he has sensed the confrontation of the great
hostile power : public order, the law, Jerusalem.
Thus had he seen the emissaries of the Sanhedrim
confronting John ; blaming and cross-examining ;
the messengers of men in face of the messenger of
God.   It was with the same sour expression as the
one they wore to-day, that they had looked into
the burning eyes of the Baptist.   Then, as now,
the enquiry had been emphasised by a pointing
of the forefinger.   Jesus and those who took him
to task, like the Baptist and the Pharisees on that
earlier day, were surrounded by a gaping crowd.
John's figure and face, John's dark and tangled
locks, rise before his mind's eye ; and at the same
time Jesus recalls the Baptist's words : " He that
cometh after me is mightier than I."   He recalls,
likewise, John's recent question : " Art thou he
that should come, or do we look for another ? "
Thereupon, the self-confidence which, during his
flight, had been repressed into silence, wells up
in him once more ; the longing to grapple with
his enemies in the open has its way with him.
The boy's ancient dislike of the self-righteous
mingles with the tensions of the present situation.
A direct answer to the ludicrous query is hardly
worth while.   Into these innocent hands there
would seem, of a sudden, to be thrust an invisible
weapon.   With the ringing voice of the Baptist,
he challenges his adversaries in the market
place :

" Why do ye also transgress the commandment
of God by your tradition ?   For God commanded,
saying : ' Honour thy father and mother ' ; and,
' He that curseth father or mother, let him die
the death.'   But ye say that he doeth well who
saith to his father and mother, ' When I offer up
to God that which I owe to you, then I am doing
much more for you !'   In such fashion, truly, no
one will any longer honour his father and his
mother !   Thus have ye made the commandment
of God of none effect by your tradition.   Ye
hypocrites, well did Isaiah prophesy of you,
saying : ' This people draweth nigh unto me with
their mouth, and honoureth me with their lips ;
but their heart is far from me.   Howbeit in vain
do they worship me, teaching for doctrines the
commandments of men.' "

In this way he brings up their own custom
against them, quotes against them the words of
their own prophets, and relieves his pent-up
feelings by charging his foes with the sin of self-
righteousness.   The shaft strikes home, it would
seem ; for they make no answer, and silently go
their way.   When they strike back, their vengeful
thrust will slay him.

Jesus, however, is in the vein.   It is long since
he has spoken to the people, and never before
with so much fire as to-day. Motioning his
auditors to close round him, in the market place
of this dusty little town he addresses the multitude

in words and manner which imply that he regards the common folk of Galilee as a court of appeal against Jerusalem. Mocking at the venerable prohibitions of certain sorts of food as unclean (prohibitions upon which the Pharisees lay especial stress), while those who have just been questioning him are still within earshot he thunders : " Hear, and understand ! Not that which goeth into the mouth defileth a man ; but that which cometh out of the mouth, this defileth a man !"

The disciples are alarmed. Never before have they seen him so much moved. Dreading a further clash with the authorities, they come up to him and say in low tones : " Knowest thou that the Pharisees were offended, after they heard thy saying ?" But he, who used to be gentle and guarded in his utterances, has now thrown caution to the winds. One metaphor chases another through his mind, and all of them are of a nature to hold up the scribes and Pharisees to scorn. His voice rings through the market place : " Every plant which my heavenly Father hath not planted, shall be rooted up. Let them alone ; they are blind leaders of the blind. If one blind man lead another, both shall fall into the ditch."

His hearers fancy they catch the sound of heathen laughter echoing from behind his back. The disciples are growing more and more uneasy. Peter, in the hope of checking him, breaks in, saying : " Explain this parable." Impatient at the interruption, Jesus answers hectoringly : " Are ye also yet without understanding ? Do not ye yet perceive, that whatsoever entereth in at the mouth goeth into the belly, and is cast out thence by the natural vent ? But those things which proceed out of the mouth, come forth from the heart ; and they may defile the man." The speaker's eyes flash fiery darts after the departing Pharisees as he goes on : " For out of the heart proceed evil thoughts, murders, adulteries, fornications, thefts, false witness, blasphemies. These are the things which defile a man ! But to eat with unwashed hands defileth not a man !"

Thus in the concluding words of his outburst, and in them only, does he answer the Pharisees' crafty question. These words mean an open breach, and Jesus has willed it. Let them make their way home, to inform the priests, to let all Jerusalem know, what the fanatical carpenter has dared to say. At least he has, before the whole people, told his deadly enemies what he thinks of them. He has burst his bonds. He is free.

II.

Larger and ever larger are the crowds that gather to hear him, the companies that follow in his train. For they pursue him, both by land and by sea, in his frequent migrations, now that he moves on more restlessly than before, and with less of a fixed purpose, often looking over his shoulder to glimpse (if he can) where the foe lies hid. It is the declared enmity of the orthodox and the strait-laced which, to begin with, brings him a larger following ; for the peasantfolk, by a natural reaction, espouse the cause of one who is in the priests' black books. Did the priests ever show a kindly thought for the troubles of the poor, ever do anything more than enjoin a strict observance of the law ? They kept themselves to themselves, as they stalked through the streets, aloof in their puritan pride. There was no such vaingloriousness about Jesus. He had always done his utmost to console the lowly in their afflictions, for he was one of themselves.

All the same, they think he may be Elijah come to life again, or another of the prophets whose advent is to be expected if happier days are in store. They never dream of regarding him as the Son of David or as the Messiah. Having faith in him as one who does good works here and now, they call him what he calls himself, the Son

of Man. Besides, they know that even the
Pharisees come to beg Jesus' help, when the need
is sore ! The very rulers of the synagogue fall
at his feet, on occasions. Here is one, Jairus,
beseeching : " My little daughter lieth at the
point of death. I pray thee, come and lay thy
hands on her, that she may be healed." Jesus
turns to go with Jairus, and the throng presses
after. At this moment, slaves rush forth from the
house saying that it is too late, for the girl is dead.
But he, who knows that the ignorant countryfolk
are too ready, in cases of grievous illness, to believe
that death has come, pays no heed. Mending
his pace, and taking with him only three of his
disciples, he enters the room where the next of
kin and the attendants are waiting, and says to
them : " Why make ye this ado, and weep ?
The damsel is not dead, but sleepeth." Some
who hear these words begin to titter, whereupon
he has the room cleared of all but the parents
and his three disciples. To Jairus, he says:
" Fear not ; only believe." Then he wakes the
child ; takes her by the hand, saying, " Maid,
arise !" and, after his manner, enforces his will
upon her, so that she gets up from what had
seemed to be her deathbed.

All are astonished and affrighted. This man,
who can bring the dead back to life, must be
a sorcerer of the most formidable kind ! His
skill as a healer, which at first had smoothed his

path, again opens a gulf (as it had done at Gadara) between him and the common people. To begin with, it was as a physician that he won hearts ; now, it is by his powers as a physician that he sets hearts against him.

Discouraged, he stands before this people upon which he has lavished so much love and so much patience. He cannot but think of the woman of Samaria, the Gentile who, in contrast with these children of Israel, had broken down his own unwillingness by her unflinching faith. He begins upbraiding the multitude, to which hitherto he has ever wished to bring solace. In his new and wrathful tone, he exclaims : " Woe unto thee, Chorazin ! Woe unto thee Bethsaida ! For if the mighty works, which were done in you, had been done in Tyre and Sidon, they would have repented long ago in sackcloth and ashes. But I say unto you, it shall be more tolerable for Tyre and Sidon at the day of judgment than for you. And thou, Capernaum, which art exalted unto heaven, shalt be brought down to hell ; for if the mighty works which have been done in thee, had been done in Sodom, it would have remained to this day."

Those who stand round him, listening to his words, shake their heads dubiously. He had been wont to talk to them like a shepherd ; now he talks to them like John the Baptist. Can it be the same man ? Why does he speak to us so

much about the heathen? Why does he boast
of his wonderful deeds, which nobody wants to
deny? When he wrought miraculous cures, he
used to charge those whom he had made whole
that they should tell no man.

No less disappointed in the dull-witted populace
than he is inflamed with anger against the guardians of the law, he tends increasingly to draw
away from both. Though the urge is but half
conscious, he is more and more inclined to bid
farewell to Galilee, and to wander into the
lands of the heathen. Sometimes he crosses the
southern frontier into Samaria, sometimes he
oversteps the north-western border and makes his
way towards Tyre. In either case it is to aid the
Gentiles, whom he cures without teaching them
and without even trying to convert them. No
doubt it was among Gentiles that he heard the
tale (the incident may have been one of his
experiences of travel) which he told in answer
to the question: "Who is my neighbour, whom
I should love even as myself?" Jesus answered,
gently enough this time: " A certain man on the
road from Jerusalem to Jericho fell among
thieves, who stripped him of his raiment, and
wounded him, and departed, leaving him half
dead. And by chance there came a priest that
way, and after him a Levite ; but both of them,
seeing the despoiled traveller lying helpless in
the road, passed by on the other side. Then

came a man from Samaria, a heathen, who, perceiving the wounded stranger, had compassion on him, bound up his wounds, set the man on his own mule, brought him to an inn, and paid the host to care for him till he should be well again. Which now, of these three, thinkest thou, was neighbour unto him that fell among the thieves ? . . . Go thou and do likewise." And because millions upon millions have told Jesus' tale after him, the kindly deed of the nameless Samaritan has immortalised the name of the little heathen people to which he belonged.

Persecuted, despised (for Jesus cannot fail to recognise that such is his fate), he holds aloof from the multitude, and consorts only with his disciples. They shall learn his thoughts, and disseminate that which no longer commands universal credence when it comes direct from the mouth of one who is a mark for so much criticism. The more the world forces him into retirement, the more, by slow degrees, does his doctrine take shape in his inward personality, in the realm of feeling, without any rigid precepts or set forms of expression. Of course, he cannot always speak to them lovingly, as a father speaks to his children ; he is also their master, and must command. All the bitterness of a man whose nature is childlike in its simplicity, one who had tried to find his way openly and frankly into the hearts of all, only to encounter the chill resistance of an unsympathetic world ; this disillusionment is what breathes from his counsel to the disciples (whom he also speaks of as his apostles) : "Behold I send you forth as sheep in the midst of wolves : be ye therefore wise as serpents, and guileless as doves !" Truly he himself has always been without guile, but the cunning of the serpent has never been his. Now Jesus has become father to his disciples, and the children, profiting by his experience, are to show more wisdom than he.

At the same time he is determined that there shall be no question of his founding a religious order, like that of the Essenes. There are to be no insignia ; and he asks harder things of his disciples than any such as he has asked before him. On their journeyings they are to take with them no money, nor bread, nor pilgrim's wallet, nor even a staff. Like himself, they will find persons ready to provide them with food whithersoever they go. Those whose mission is to the poor and the defenceless, must themselves be poor and defenceless. "And whosoever will not receive you, when ye go out of that city, shake off the very dust from your feet for a testimony against them. But when they persecute you in one city, flee ye into another." How harsh the once gentle teacher has become ! Where are the loving tones of his earlier days ?

We seem to be listening to the voice of one who is nothing but an embittered prophet.

When the disciples behave foolishly, he speaks to them thus : " Why call ye me ' Master, Master,' and do not the things which I say ? When ye shall say, ' We have eaten and drunk in thy presence, and thou hast taught in our streets '; then he shall say, ' I know you not, whence you are ; depart from me all ye workers of iniquity !' " Thus remote does he already feel from his most trusty pupils. When new aspirants approach him, he speaks to them overbearingly : " If any man come to me and hate not his father, and mother, and wife, and children, and brethren, and sisters, yea, and his own life also, he cannot be my disciple."

Once, to a man who pleases him, he says curtly : " Follow me."

" Lord," answers the stranger, "suffer me first to bury my father."

" Let the dead bury their dead ! Come thou and preach the kingdom of God !"

From another, whom he has told to follow him, and who has asked leave to go home first, to bid farewell, he turns away contemptuously, saying : " No man, having put his hand to the plough, and looking back, is fit for the kingdom of God."

So fanatical, already, is the man who had not long since reproached the Pharisees on the ground that their rules hindered a son from doing his duty to his father.

Jesus even goes to the extreme of publicly disowning his mother. Wishing to make one more attempt to wean her son from his present dangerous courses, she seeks him out, bringing with her her other sons, to assist in the work of persuasion. They send in a message, saying they wish to see him. He is told, " Behold thy mother and thy brethren are without." Thereupon he says to his disciples : "Who is my mother, or my brethren ?   You are my mother and my brethren. For whosoever shall do the will of God, the same is my brother, and my sister, and my mother."

Only from time to time does he give utterance to the serene and delightful wisdom of earlier days.   Once when he hears the disciples disputing among themselves as to which of them will be greatest in the kingdom of heaven, he sits down on a rock by the wayside, silently hiding his disappointment at so crude an interpretation of his teaching.   Then, catching sight of a little boy at play in the road, he calls the child to him. Taking the youngster on his knee he says to the surrounding company : " Verily I say unto you, except ye be changed, and become as little children, ye shall not enter into the kingdom of heaven. Whosoever, therefore, shall humble himself as this little child, the same is greatest in the kingdom of heaven."

III.

There is high festival in the fortress of Machærus. It is Herod's birthday, and the tetrarch has invited the lords, the high captains, and the chief estates of Galilee, to celebrate the occasion. He knows naught of the schemes that are a-hatching behind his back.

For a long time, the chief priests in Jerusalem have been urging him to make an end of the man who is in duress below, the man whose name and influence have been magnified by imprisonment. Above all, they hope that the slaughter of John will intimidate the Nazarene, John's pupil, round whom so many of the Baptist's followers have gathered, and who seems to be leading the sectaries into dangerous paths. Herod has always rejected these promptings. As a states-man, he knows that a martyr's memory may be more dangerous than the repute of a living prophet ; as a philosopher, he enjoys an occasional talk with John ; as a weakling, he dreads the consequences of a murder which will profit no one.

Herodias, who outdoes her husband both in courage and in the power of sustained hatred, lends a ready ear to the messages from the Sanhedrim. The prisoner's strictures on her marriage may not seriously threaten the integrity

of her union with the tetrarch, but they
are none the less wounding to her pride. The
Pharisees and the Sadducees are quick to discover this mortified self-love, and to turn it to
account for their own political ends. Herodias
has promised to work John's destruction, and
has drawn her daughter, Salome, into the plot.
Salome has recently lost her husband, the
tetrarch Philip, who was well on in years. The
widow is young, full of life and vigour, and the
fame of her skill as a dancer has spread even to
distant Rome.

To-day, schooled by her mother, she dances
in the banqueting hall, dances before the assembled officers and State officials ; but above
all before Herod, her stepfather, who loves anything that can, even for a moment, revive a glow
in the embers of his vanished youth. As he
reclines at the board, heated with wine, and the
dancing ends at midnight, he hears the thunders
of applause, notes the lustful glances of the
courtiers and the demure approval of the waiting
slaves ; he fixes his gaze on the central figure
of the scene—the lithe dancer, half-naked, looking more like a harlot than a princess, who has
been footing it so merrily to the accompaniment
of lutes and pipes. There awakens in him the
old wish of the oriental despot to make a parade
of his largesse, to pay homage to beauty by a
display of his generosity and his power and his

wealth. It may well be that Herodias (who in general is loath to flaunt her daughter's fresh young charms before the weary Herod) has to-night given her husband a hint to show special favour to the heroine of the hour. His thoughts naturally turn to Esther, one of the favourite personalities in the Jewish folk tales. The ambitious ruler would be glad to start a new legend, which would depict himself as a figure no less magnificent than Ahasuerus had been in days of old. That is why he now addresses Salome in Ahasuerus' words : " Ask of me whatsoever thou wilt, and I will give it thee. Whatsoever thou shalt ask of me, I will give it thee, unto the half of my kingdom."

The hearers spring to their feet, for they know that this is a critical moment, and wonder what the dancer will ask. Strings of pearls for wrist and ankles ? A town, perhaps ; or even half a province ? Why does she proffer her request in tones so low that none but the tetrarch can hear ? Is it something unseemly ? Look, Herod turns pale, staggers away from the table, claps a hand to his heart. What in the name of wonder can she have asked for ? None of them know, but they see that Herodias' eyes are bright with triumphant joy. The tetrarch has quitted the hall.

In a neighbouring apartment, Herod sits alone, gasping for breath, communing with his

own thoughts. The head of John the Baptist!
Is not a temptation of God hidden behind the
pretty dancer's veil? Why not offer her something else? He sends for Salome, questions her,
implores her. But her mother's strict injunctions and her own feelings of cruelty tinged with
lust combine to steel her determination. She
will not budge. He offers her a city, a province.
No, she wants neither the one nor the other.
Nothing will content her but what she first asked
for, John the Baptist's head upon a golden
charger. He tries in vain to win over Herodias.
She must induce her daughter to give way. Here
the tetrarch encounters a chilly silence. Well,
after all, why should he not grant the request
to which his word is pledged? The man
prisoned in the crypt is a poor visionary, the
enemy of the rich and the powerful, detested
by the learned. Why should John be spared?
By the waters of Jordan he had been a preacher
of revolt, had laid his plans for a rising.

Herod gives a sign to his slaves, and orders
the music to cease.

No one knows what has happened, or what
is about to happen. Some of the guests are
speechless, others exchange tense whispers.
Their wine is left untouched. Herod is trying
to nerve himself for what is coming. Now there
are heavy footfalls on the stair. Armed men
stride in, and behind them comes one bearing,

on a golden charger, the head of John the Baptist. The executioner carries the head to Salome. At first she shrinks from the grisly object ; then, plucking up courage, she takes the charger in her own hands and presents it to her mother.

The news spread quickly throughout the country, producing general alarm. There had recently been other ominous signs. In especial, panic prevailed in Galilee, for a number of un- ruly persons from that province (zealots, and sometime followers of Judas the Galilean), stirred to action by the Messianic rumours of the time, had made a raid into Jerusalem, where they had insulted the Romans and attacked the temple guard. Pilate had had them all arrested. One of these disturbers of the peace bore, so it was said, the name of Barabbas. Even Jesus, in some out-of-the-way corner, had heard the tidings from the capital. Since in his then state of mind everything that happened seemed to him significant in relation to his own mission, he had believed the affair to be the prelude to a general uprising. Another incident that aggravated his nervous tension at this moment was the fall of a tower hard by the pool of Siloam, a disaster resulting in eighteen deaths.

Then the disciples bring him the news of John's execution. Sorrow overwhelms Jesus. Vivid images course through his mind : the supreme moment beside the waters of Jordan ; John

imprisoned ; John slain !   The lucidity of spiritual
illumination returns in a flash, as of lightning,
which is followed by a deafening clap of thunder.
Again his great exemplar points the way.   From
the very crypt of the prison, the dead Baptist's
voice still seems to call : " He that cometh after
me is mightier than I."

" He that cometh after me !"   Is it his fate to
follow in John's footsteps to the end ?   The
question gallops stormily through his mind.   The
path, which he would gladly have seen taken by
another than himself, has been cleared irrevo-
cably ; the last pretext for inaction, the last
excuse for hesitation have been removed ; all the
imaginings with which he has been obsessed
during the last few weeks, clamour for realisation
in the world of fact.

For the fourth time it is John who drives him
forward on the road leading towards an unknown
goal.   The story of the baptisms beside Jordan
had lured him from a tranquil life in the mountain village of Nazareth, had brought him into
contact with the multitude ; when the arrest
had taken place, the prisoner's mission had
devolved upon himself ; the momentous question
sent from Machærus had awakened the slumbering Messiah ; to-day, John's death came as a new
message to Jesus, a summons to open avowal.
But this enigmatic consecration, at the same time
disclosed the way of suffering.

Again terror seizes the man thus singled out.
Again he believes that he is listening to the voice
of the Father ; but this time the voice thunders,
and no dove descends as a sign of rapturous
days to come. Danger threatens from Herod,
who is determined to slay every innovator ;
persecution from the Pharisees, who will now feel
confident of the tetrarch's favour and protection.
Yet in his heart of hearts there is a raging thirst ;
the thirst of one who feels that he himself is
chosen ; the longing to pay a debt to the people,
to his own self, to God—by fulfilling the supreme
charge which has thus been laid upon him.

Awe-stricken, Jesus, with his disciples, flees
eastward across the lake, and thence northward,
to the foot of Mount Hermon.

IV.

On the left bank of Jordan, a wide and fertile
valley ascends to the foothills. Here the river
is scarce twenty paces wide, still turbulent and
young. From Jordan, looking up this lateral
valley, the traveller sees the fortress of Cæsarea
Philippi, and the fine new town that surrounds
it. Here, till recently, Herod Philip had reigned,
a man of peaceful disposition, the husband of
that Salome whose dancing had cost the Baptist
his head. Perchance had Philip lived longer

and kept Salome by his side, John's life would
have been spared, and another life besides ; it
may well be that Jesus would not have been
storm-driven into this northern port.

Here, as the fugitive well knows, had been the
frontier of Israel in the old days, when Israel
was free and powerful. No Jewish sovereign,
not even David, had held sway farther north
than this. Now the region is inhabited by Greeks
and other heathen. Standing by the upper waters
of Jordan, his eye follows the strange river in its
precipitous southward course ; on, on, in imagination, to where it flows into the Dead Sea. He
thinks of all that has happened since he met
John. February has come again ; this year has
been for him more eventful than the whole of
the previous thirty years. How many remain to
be lived ? The spring of life and its close, the
source of Jordan and its end only a hundred
miles away, where John had baptised him—is
this a parable for him to read ? John has been
slain.

Beyond the town, still accompanied by his
disciples, he comes to the spot which the pagans
regard as the source of Jordan. Here there is
a cave, dedicated to Pan. Round about are
votive tablets, marble statues, Greek inscriptions.
A man from Philippi, passing that way and seeing
the strangers in the grotto, comes and explains
everything to Jesus. This statue represents the

nymph who lives in the spring ; those others are
the river spirits ; that one over there, the most
beautiful of all, is Echo.   It is she who carries
the voice from rock to rock when you shout—as
the exponent now shouts in illustration.   Everything belongs to Great Pan, who rules all that
lies betwixt air and water.   Sometimes the
herdsmen catch a glimpse of him, in the noontide sun, when he lies asleep naked, upon
a rock.   The disciples, glancing for a moment
at the carven images of the nymphs, are shocked,
and turn away their eyes, lest temptation should
overpower them.

Jesus, however, looks at everything, and listens
attentively to all that the heathen stranger has
to say.   Then, leaving the cave, he lies down in
the shade.   He has heard, often enough, about
these graven images of gods ; but this is the first
time that news has come to him of Pan, to whom
the grotto and the spring have been consecrated.
Yet of Pan there is no image.   Maybe he is
a spirit.   If he rules all that lies betwixt air and
water, he has perhaps wandered in the hills of
Nazareth ere now.   If he be a bodiless spirit, how
can the herdsmen see him ? Jesus has himself,
when tending sheep, heard the voice of nature,
the soughing of the wind, the murmur of the
foliage, the rustling of the grass ; but no great
earth spirit has he ever seen.   The voice was the
voice of his Father in heaven, not the voice of Pan.

It seems so long ago since he was as callow as these young fellows, his disciples ! How dull-witted they are ; how little they can understand ! They scarcely know whom they are following, to whom they are giving ear. How can they know, unless he reveals himself to them ? He must question them, must put them to the test. If the conviction that has filled his mind since hearing of John's death should be a false belief, inspired by the devil, then the disciples will certainly fail to acknowledge him as the Messiah. Nay, even if the conviction comes from God, they may still fail to acknowledge him. God alone can awaken their drowsy senses ; will he do so ?

After these musings, Jesus turns to the disciples and asks them : " Whom do men say that I am?"

Each one of them has an answer ready ; the answers are all different : " Some say that thou art John the Baptist ; some, Elijah ; and others, Jeremiah, or one of the prophets."

They dispute among themselves, as to which of these answers may be right. They do not know. Shall he venture upon the decisive, the great, the hazardous, question ? Will one among the twelve give him the answer ? Perhaps to ask at all will be to tempt God. Even as he thinks this, the urge masters him, and he says, almost in spite of himself :

" Whom say ye that I am ?"

They are silent, embarrassed ; some of them

keep their eyes fixed on the ground. All but one
are afraid to utter their thoughts. It is Peter,
the most impulsive among them, who plucks
up courage, looks him in the face, and says :
" Thou art the Messiah !"

A beam of light glorifies Jesus' world. At length
has been spoken the fateful word ; the word
for which he has been waiting, amid wrestlings
of soul, since John's enquiry : " Art thou he
that should come ?" Through the magic of this
utterance, the feelings that have so long been
cherished in the loneliness of his heart break
forth, and suffuse the day with sunshine.
Acknowledged by another, he wins for the first
time full confidence in himself. Spreading his
arms wide, he gives Peter a benediction more
enthusiastic than any other that has been re-
corded of him : " Blessed art thou, Simon son of
Jonas : for flesh and blood hath not revealed it
unto thee, but my Father which is in heaven."
A moment later he is rueful because the hoarded
secret has been disclosed, and he adjures the
disciples to tell no one that he, Jesus, is the
Christ.

His impulse towards discretion comes too late !
The open declaration, the stir of the time, persecution, pride, renewed courage—all drive him
forward along the path of the man elect. What
can the Messiah do here among the heathen, on
the northernmost verge of the realm ? Nor is

there any fitting work left for him in little Galilee.
He must go to the place he has hitherto so
persistently shunned ; he must go to Jerusalem,
and conquer it ! The Feast of the Passover is
at hand ; Jews from all parts of the world will be
assembled in the capital. The hour has struck !
It is there that the Messiah must deliver his
message, as the prophets have foretold !

Calling the disciples closer, in low tones he
discloses his purpose. He must go to Jerusalem,
and there be put to death.

A shudder runs round the circle of listeners.
They have never dreamed of his going to this
length, and such a fulfilment of the ancient
writings seems to them lunacy. Only one of
them ventures to utter his thoughts. Peter,
straightforward as usual, takes the master by the
arm and exclaims : " Be it far from thee, Lord !
This shall not be unto thee !"

Jesus feels that they do not understand him,
not even the man whom, but now, he had thought
to have been singled out as the recipient of God's
illumination. Have none of his faithful followers
grasped the supreme mystery which he guardedly
revealed to them when the word Messiah was
spoken ? Do they think of nothing more than
bread and sleep, and perhaps a little sermon-
ising in addition ? He shakes off Peter's restrain-
ing hand, and says fiercely : " Get thee behind
me, Satan ! Thou art an offence to me : for

thou savourest not the things that be of God, but those that be of men !"

They leap to their feet and stand gazing at him, with mingled feelings of awe and repulsion. He has apostrophised Peter as " Satan " ; Peter, their favourite. In his passionate rejection of Peter's dissuasion, he had seemed to grow in stature. Their wrathful leader does, in very truth, look like one of the prophets of old ! Jesus, facing them, bolder than ever before, a fighter, resolute to meet his fate, speaks as follows :

" If any man will come after me, let him deny himself, and take up his cross and follow me. For whosoever will save his life, shall lose it ; but whosoever shall lose his life for my sake and the gospel's, the same shall save it. What shall it profit a man, if he gain the whole world, and lose his own soul ? Or what shall a man give in exchange for his soul? Whosoever therefore shall be ashamed of me and of my words in this sinful generation ; of him also shall the Son of Man be ashamed, when he cometh in the glory of his Father with the holy angels. Verily I say unto you : there be some that stand here who shall not taste of death till they have seen the kingdom of God come in its power."

With princely mien, Jesus turns about and sets forth on his way.

14

V.

" He that is not for me, is against me !"

Such is the new word of the prophet who, having returned home for a brief space, is preparing to go to Jerusalem. For Jesus has at length become a man of battle. He has hesitated long. Gentle and imaginative, a poet by temperament, a teacher who lives to bring cheer and consolation, a compassionate physician, the more strenuous way has not seemed to him God's will, and has certainly not been his own. But the smouldering quarrel between himself and his brethren has broken into flame. The great Father, whom Jesus hitherto has always represented as full of love, must decide the issue between the righteous and the unrighteous among his children.

Not among them all ! Now that he feels himself to be the Messiah, now that he has openly announced his Messianic mission, now that he has informed the disciples that he is fulfilling the ancient prophecies, ecstasy has taken full possession of him. All he can think of, henceforward, is that it lies with him to fulfil what the scriptures have foretold. The Son is no longer one among many loving sons who are all equally dear to the Father's heart. He is the Chosen One, the Unique, the Mediator, the

Judge. The quiet and peaceful days are over. The kingdom of heaven, whose coming he has so long proclaimed, is indeed at hand ; it is coming with a great assize, amid alarums and excursions ; and, as a prelude, that all the prophecies may be fulfilled, the redeemer of the world must be despitefully used by his enemies, be condemned by them and put to a shameful death.

Therewith a great barrier rises between teacher and disciples, between the strolling preacher and his congregations, between Jesus and the world. His conversation with God becomes a mystery. Pride surges up from within, breaking through the tender restraints of a heart which from childhood upwards has been unexampled in its humility—as if in a deliberate endeavour to counteract the impulses that now rise to the surface. Masterfulness and judgeship ; loftiness and solitary grandeur ; the poise of mind natural to one who is convinced that he has a world mission, in conjunction with the resolve to face the sacrificial death that will glorify him : all these combine to make him more virile, more reserved, more sombre, than any who had known him by his past record—by his teaching, his courteous gestures, his kindly glance, his gentle words—could ever have deemed possible.

When he and his company are still upon the homeward road, there comes a stormy afternoon

when he gives a sign to his three favourite
disciples, Peter, James, and John. Leaving the
others, they climb a high mountain where some
of the greatest of the prophets had dwelt. In
this remote spot, he can steep himself in their
spirit, can listen to their counsel. The mists
thicken as the four go up, the light is failing, and
they can scarcely see farther than the next tree.
At a little distance, the human figure, almost
vanishing in the cloud-wraiths, seems strangely
magnified. The three disciples, uncertain and
timid, draw closer together. The master has
all but disappeared from their ken. He is no
more than one of the white wraiths, as it were
transfigured where he stands apart. They are
weary, and, lying down, they fall asleep.

Then, in a dream, Peter sees the two prophets,
Moses and Elijah, with whom, these days, his
thoughts have been filled. They are talking
with Jesus. Ever since the hour when the
master was revealed to him as the Messiah, he
has been seeking a way out of the dangers that
threaten. A man of shrewd common sense,
he thinks he has found what he needs, and, still
dreaming, he calls out : " Rabbi, it is good for
us to be here. Let us make three huts, one for
thee, and one for Moses, and one for Elijah."
With a sudden transition, the dreamer's thoughts
fly back to what Jesus had told them of his
mission, and to the undercurrent of his own

doubts. The answer to these doubts takes audible shape, and the sleeping Peter seems to hear a distant voice, uttering the very words which Jesus had heard immediately after the baptism in Jordan : " This is my beloved Son, in whom I am well pleased. Hear him !"

Betwixt sleep and waking, Peter leaps to his feet, and then throws himself on the ground, hiding his face. James and John, roused by his words and movements, do the same thing, for they too are sore afraid. In the mist, on this sacred mount, at any moment God may appear in all his glory ! When, after a while, they venture to raise their heads from the ground, Jesus is standing before them, saying quietly : " Rise up, and fear nothing !" In the earlier tones he had been wont to use before his recent access of spiritual pride, he charges them to tell no man of the things they have seen.

Soon, however, when they have gone down from the mountain and are again by the lake shore, the influences that had transformed him of late resume their sway. The curiosity of the common folk, the hostile glances of his enemies, the passing of the pilgrims on the way to the festival at Jerusalem, renew his determination to act as befits his Messianic mission. His every word becomes a command ; his every command a threat. He says to his disciples : " He that heareth you, heareth me ; he that despiseth you, despiseth me ; and he that despiseth me, despiseth him that sent me !" Again : " Whosoever shall confess me before men, him will I confess also before my Father which is in heaven. But whosoever shall deny me before men, him will I also deny before my Father which is in heaven." When they are unsuccessful in their attempt to cure a lunatic boy, he rails at them thus : " O faithless and perverse that ye are, how long shall I be with you, how long shall I suffer you ?"

Herod's tax-gatherers come to demand the dues, the tribute, from him and his followers. Peter, to whom they have applied, asks the master what is to be done. Comes in answer, this question :

" What thinkest thou, Simon ? Of whom do the kings of the earth take custom or tribute ? Of their own children, or of strangers ?"

" Of strangers, Lord."

" Then are the children free."

He now has a king's sense of self-importance, and is affronted that the State should make claims on him, as if he were but a citizen like any other. Still, with a remnant of prudence he bethinks himself that he must avoid giving his enemies a new handle against him, for his youthful memories of the fate of Judas the Galilean are ever in his mind as a warning of what happens to those who defy the authority of the State.

He therefore finds an expedient for paying the taxes after all.

But, for the very reason that he has neither desire for nor expectation of temporal splendour, he, who has never devoted thought or effort to the things of this world, fancies that mere faith in himself, the mere conviction of his mission, will suffice—without plan, and without search for definite means—to bring about a general spiritual rebirth. Living in a theocracy which for hundreds of years has taught the coming of the Messiah, and now, under the Roman rule, is passionately expecting the advent of this deliverer, he now builds upon his own conviction that he is the redeemer. Surely his pure and passionate sense that he is the chosen of God must communicate itself to those to whom he discloses himself? Thus it is that he, who has always extolled love and reasonableness, who has never advocated any attempt to subvert the existing social order, now drifts day by day nearer to perilous whirlpools.

Daily, he magnifies the conception of his predestined role. He is greater than Abraham or Solomon. He says : "All things are delivered unto me from my Father : and no man knoweth the Son but the Father; neither knoweth any man the Father, save the Son, and he to whomsoever the Son will reveal him." The tender feeling of a filial relationship towards an all-loving Father, has given place to an arrogant ecstasy, as though he alone were loved by the Father and could know the Father. Nay more, his lust of battle, generalised, but vacillating in its aim, inspires him with the vengeful thoughts of the old prophets, thoughts which before were uncongenial to him. He lashes himself on with savage words, as if he had to out-voice the promptings of his truer self : " I am come to send fire on the earth ; all the better, therefore, if it be already kindled ! . . . Suppose ye that I am come to give peace on earth ? I tell you, nay ; but, rather, division. For from henceforth there shall be five in one house divided, three against two, and two against three. The father shall be divided against the son, and the son against the father ; the mother against the daughter, and the daughter against the mother."

John's fate has taught him that to-day, just as in ancient times, God lets his prophets suffer and perish. He is familiar with the expiatory careers of Abraham, Moses, and Job. Yet he is in love with life, and strives for victory. At times, he declares that he wants to die, in order that he may found the kingdom of heaven; at times, he appears to seek out suffering, to take a strange delight in the persecution that dogs his footsteps ; at times, he seems to think fulfil-ment at hand, and hindered only by wicked men. That is why his mind turns so eagerly to thoughts of resurrection followed by a last judgment; and, since he cannot escape the foreboding that death is drawing very near, he cherishes imaginative pictures of a world beyond the grave, in which he will triumph.

Resurrection, taught by Daniel and Enoch, though not an article of faith with all the Jews, is to Jesus a palpable reality. At board, over the wine, he talks of the future life. Sometimes it is only a boon for the righteous. At other times it is also a threat for the unrighteous, a state in which the ungodly will for the first time get their deserts. Assuredly there will be a day of judgment, though none may know when that day will dawn. For the day of the Lord will come like a thief in the night, like a lightning-flash on the horizon; and the Father alone knoweth at what hour. When the master wishes to encourage his disciples, he tells them that the kingdom of heaven will come while they can still see it with the eyes of the flesh. Thus uncertain, thus conflicting, are Jesus' words upon a matter which is beyond the range of his kindlier human feelings, and forcibly superimposed on them.

One thing only is he sure of, and that is his own place in heaven. Daniel, his favourite teacher, had beheld one like to the Son of Man coming with the clouds of heaven, coming to the Ancient of Days. This supplies him with the

imagery for his own description of what awaits
him. On the throne, at the right hand of the
Father, he will sit during the last judgment;
and when the great assize is over, he will rule
for ever and ever. The power which, as the
scripture tells us, God has hitherto kept jealously
to himself, will then be given to the Son : " For
the Father judgeth no man, but hath committed
all judgment unto the Son, that all men should
honour the Son, even as they honour the
Father." This being so, he is to-day already
empowered to judge and to rule; an authority
such as no one before him has ever believed
himself to possess, entitles him to choose some
and reject others.

" Verily, verily, I say unto you, he that heareth
my word, and believeth on him that sent me,
hath everlasting life, and shall not come into
condemnation." Yet the same man says, in the
same discourse : " I can of mine own self do
nothing. As I hear, I judge ; and my judgment
is just ; because I seek not mine own will, but the
will of the Father which has sent me."

Such are the menaces and the exuberances,
the jubilations and the comminations, of his
Messianic ecstasies. A placid carpenter, full
of God's grace, overflowing with love for the
heavenly Father, for his earthly brethren, for
children, animals, and plants, has, by stress of
the popular demand that he should work

miracles, by the acclamations of the multitude, by the suspicion and enmity of the priests, by the contempt of his family and the adulation of his disciples, by the sayings and the doings and the fate of a forerunner, been driven within a year along a narrowing and steepening path, until at length he has come to believe that he is the redeemer whom a proud and suffering people awaits, to bring deliverance and afterwards to rule. The battlefield had seemed so small at first, the grounds of difference so trifling. The dispute turned upon the plucking of a few ears of corn on the Sabbath, upon the washing of hands before meat, upon converse with publicans and sinners. Never had the new prophet urged the people to disregard commandments, to ignore formulas, to neglect sacrifices, even though such things were personally distasteful to him. What had severed him from his opponents cut far deeper than rites and ceremonies, but was not a matter censurable in words; it was a matter of innermost feeling.

Now, however, when this same man proclaimed himself the Messiah, declared himself of like nature with God, shook the main pillars of Moses' temple, the affair had come to a new pass. The foundations of the theocracy were menaced. No State authority can tolerate the activities of one who seems to be an impostor, or at best a madman. The high priest was at length seriously enraged, and with good reason. News came that the man of Nazareth, returning to the synagogue of Capernaum where he had begun his mission, had openly declared: " I am the bread of life. He that cometh to me, shall never hunger ; and he that believeth in me, shall never thirst. . . . For I came down from heaven, not to do mine own will, but the will of him that sent me. . . . And this is the will of him that sent me, that every one who seeth the Son, and believeth in him, may have everlasting life, and I will raise him up at the last day."

The Jews had murmured at him, because of the words : " I am the bread which came down from heaven." They had said : " Is not this Jesus, the son of Joseph, whose father and mother we know. How is it then that he saith, ' I came down from heaven '? "

Jesus, however, had repeated the words, a second time and a third, strengthening his asseverations as he did so, until many of his disciples had said : " This is a hard saying. Who can accept it ?" But the prophet, knowing that his own pupils were among the doubters, had looked at them triumphantly, and had exclaimed : " Doth this offend you ? What and if ye shall see the Son of Man ascend up where he was before ? It is the spirit that quickeneth ; the flesh profiteth nothing. The words that I speak unto you, they are spirit and they are life. But there are some of you that believe not." Thereupon many of those who had, till then, followed him faithfully, went back, and walked no more with him. The people said : " He hath a devil !"

Within three days all these things were known to the Great Council in Jerusalem, for the word had gone forth to send prompt and full reports. Herod, too, had been warned. When the tetrarch learned that the Nazarene was openly claiming to be the Messiah, his heart blenched. Some of the potentate's courtiers, themselves uneasy, said : " Surely he must be Elijah !" But Herod, breaking in, angry and terrified, exclaimed : " Nay, it is John whom I beheaded. He is risen from the dead, and therefore mighty works do show forth themselves in him !"

As soon as the news reaches them, the Pharisees join up the threads from Machærus to Jerusalem, and from Jerusalem to Capernaum. Certain of their emissaries come to Jesus, saying : " Get thee out, and depart hence : for Herod will kill thee !"

Now is the moment when the sense of a royal mission, which has confused his better judgment, decides the issue. These crafty words are whispered in his ears. He looks into the shifty eyes of his enemies. His disciples do not understand him ; the multitude thinks him mad ; the Romans and Herod ring him round. In the holy and unholy city, which he has shunned all his life but can reach in three days—there or nowhere, now

or never, he must fight. The report is bruited
abroad that the stargazers have announced the
first day of the month of Nisan. The Passover,
therefore, is at hand. Thousands of malcontents
will flock to the capital, awaiting one who can
give them a lead. He has no clear vision of
what he will do ; but somehow, he is confident,
the general unrest of the people and the season
will decide his course for him. With kingly
demeanour he faces those who feign a wish to
save him, and rejoins :

" Go ye and tell that fox, behold, I cast out
devils, and I do cures to-day and to-morrow, and
the third day I shall come to an end. Nevertheless I must walk to-day and to-morrow, and the
day following. For it cannot be that a prophet
perish out of Jerusalem !"

CHAPTER FOUR

STRUGGLE

I.

THE shrill cries of the traders ring through the narrow streets of the great city, and are echoed by the stone walls of the houses. Barbers make a clatter with shaving utensils ; so do cobblers with the heels of slippers ; so do perfumers with copper bowls. The axles of the great wains creak ; the mules groan under the thwacking of the slaves ; the wagoners quarrel when there is a block at a street corner. With martial clank, a company of Roman soldiers forces its way through the press ; whereupon the fruit-sellers mutter curses because their baskets have been overturned, kicked dogs yelp pitifully, and terrified children bawl. To flavour the confusion in the steep and winding ways, there is a medley of evil smells, for the noontide sun of April is fierce, and, under its rays, dropped melon-rinds and other garbage fester apace ; the gulleys are choked ; from thousands of kitchens comes the reek of hot mutton-fat and of cakes that are baking ; the pungent odours from the excrement of men and beasts mingle with those of incense

and of myrrh—and all these smells are compacted
to render yet more oppressive the sweltering
atmosphere that, without a breath of wind to
stir it, hangs over the town like a canopy.

When the pilgrims who, in such multitudes,
have flocked to Jerusalem for the Passover, make
their way back from the central quarters into the
outskirts, they find in these a better air, it is true,
but no less noise ; for to-day, which is the last
Friday before the festival begins, belated caravans
are still arriving, made up of persons eager to
participate in the tumultuous celebrations. The
Feast of the Passover has a double intent : to
commemorate the deliverance out of Egypt ;
and to give thanks for the first harvest of the year.
Fallen anew into servitude, the Jews show redoubled zeal in their tribute to the glorious days
of old. It is in the north-western suburbs that
the throngs of pilgrims and of idlers from the city
are densest, for here the road from Jericho crosses
the saddle between the Mount of Olives and
the Mount of Offence. This is the highway
from the Province, and the dwellers in the
capital sally forth along it to greet the relatives
who come, year by year, to join in the eating
of the paschal lamb. As the trains of pilgrims
draw nearer to Jerusalem, they are more closely
aggregated on the converging roads ; and here,
less than an hour from the journey's end, the
procession is almost continuous, while those who

have flocked out to welcome the newcomers line
the whole route.

A crowd of idlers—citizens of Jerusalem who
have seen it all so often before, accompanied by
friends or strangers who arrived but yesterday
and would fain see the new arrivals of to-day—
has sauntered yet farther afield, to a spot whence
the houses of the Holy City are no longer visible,
and where the desert stretches away on either
hand. Of a sudden these sightseers, open-eyed
in their astonishment, behold something which
makes them crowd together and block the road.
For, preceded and followed by carts, by horses
and mules and camels carrying men and women
and their baggage, travelworn and dusty, pilgrims
of the familiar complexion, comes a strange
group, differing greatly from the ruck.

Singing, calling joyously to one another, come
these Galileans, recognisable as such by their
long hair ; a few dozen men and a sprinkling of
women, looking keenly at everything as they
pass, and dancing along, rather than walking
in the ordinary fashion. Some of them have
broken off branches from mulberry or fig trees ;
a few have shoots of palm instead. Arm-in-arm
in couples, or singly, or by threes and fours, they
advance ; not in orderly procession, but sustained by youth, and by an inward joy. They
form a setting to the central figure of their
company, to one who rides in their midst ;

15

he to whom their gestures continually draw attention.

He is mounted on a she-ass, and he looks older than his companions. Like all the others, he wears a grey cloak, soiled and shabby ; as pad for a seat, he has something bright and gay—not a folded horsecloth, but festal garments used for this purpose by his followers in order to celebrate the occasion. At its dam's heels, trots a foal, which, being thirsty, nuzzles at her occasionally from behind. Thus it is childlike in its aspect and its ways, though only the young of an ass. When the members of this little band draw near, the onlookers can at length hear the words of their song :

" Blessed be he that cometh in the name of the Lord : we have blessed you, for that you are of the house of the Lord."

Is not that the Great Hallel they sing in the temple when marching round the altar and swinging sprigs of young leaves ? Why are these wayfarers intoning a psalm which applies only to the son of David ? The listeners beckon to others, with whom they exchange questions and exclamations. Now all hear what follows :

" Rejoice greatly, O daughter of Zion ! Shout, O daughter of Jerusalem ! Behold thy King cometh unto thee, lowly, and riding upon an ass, and upon a colt the foal of an ass !"

Many of those that were listening begin to laugh. They nudge one another, saying :

"Who are these fellows? Are they mad? Do they think they are bringing the Messiah to Jerusalem?"

A crowd, growing minute by minute, attended the progress of the new group of pilgrims, who marched on undismayed, chanting their apostrophe, and swinging their green boughs.

The onlookers, meanwhile, were passing the word one to another, until all were repeating the same tale :

"'Tis a prophet—the prophet. You remember? We had news of him when a friend came from Tiberias. He is a Galilean, is Jesus the prophet of Nazareth."

From Nazareth? Is it possible, then, that these peasants do not know that the Messiah is to come out of the town of Bethlehem, and from the seed of David? What good thing ever came from Galilee? Insurgents, robbers, men possessed, yes ; there were some more of that sort from Galilee, only the other day ! But this man seems to be of a gentle disposition. It does not look as if his followers had weapons concealed about their persons. The prophet, riding on an ass, has a melancholy aspect rather than that of a warrior. Listen to the singing once more :

"Blessed be the King that cometh in the name

of the Lord : peace in heaven, and glory in the highest. Hosanna ! Alleluia !"

At first the singers had only been those of Jesus' immediate following. Now others take up the strain. The tens grow to hundreds, and the hundreds to thousands. By the time they are a mile or so nearer the town, on the over-filled high-road, there is a multitude of persons shouting and singing, though more than half of them have not the faintest idea what it is all about, and are only acting as they do under stress of the contagion of example. The disciples, however, feel this to be a triumph, and their eyes sparkle with delight. The women among them stare at the crowd, and then back at the Master, to make assurance doubly sure. " Alleluia !"

Jesus sits on his humble steed, inscrutable of countenance, looking fixedly in front of him. He takes no notice of the crowd. On the other hand, he does not interfere with his disciples, does not forbid them to acclaim him as they are doing.

Already as he left the fertile precincts of Jericho to enter the forbidding and desolate region that lies betwixt that city and Jerusalem, where all was arid and no green thing sprouted any longer, his heart misgave him. The anxiety, the terror, that he had banished during the earlier stages of the journey, now recurred in full force. The road he was travelling seemed to him the

way to prison rather than the way to the Holy
City ; and the more eagerly his disciples chattered
of their expectations, the more majestically did
he shroud himself in silence.   On reaching the
pass, however, at the village of Bethphage, when
they begged him to mount an ass even as it
had been foretold of the Messiah's coming to
Jerusalem, he realised that now, here, and to them
it would be impossible to refuse such a request ;
so he made no demur.

At length, when he is sitting on the pad made
of their cloaks, and as he watches the light-
hearted way in which (children, rather than
sages) they set themselves to the swinging of the
boughs and the chanting of the songs ; as he
listens to the psalm. and finds himself for the
first time in his life raised to the place of honour,
riding among those who go afoot, and acclaimed
beneath his Father's heaven and in all men's
ears as the Expected One ; when he sees the
movement to glorify him in this fashion spread
from his friends and intimates to casual passers-
by and to persons who have never seen him
before—then uneasy questionings assail him, and
he doubts his own purpose.

"Alleluia !" It is as the central figure in
this strange procession that he first sets eyes on
the sinister town of which he has heard so much
since earliest childhood. That place to the left,
shimmering under the midday sun, must be

Antonia, the Roman fortress. And the great building in front, somewhat ostentatious in its white purity, with its courts, its towers, and its pinnacles, its marble roof, solid-seeming as the rock on which it is builded ! That must be the temple. That is the acropolis he must conquer with the forces of the spirit ! That is the head-quarters of his foes !

Why are there no trees to glad the eyes ? There is, indeed, one green slope, one place where a spring must gush forth. But the huge city as a whole, on its rocky hills, with its strong, white walls, stands shadeless on a foundation of yellow stone, is so hard in its lines, is pitiless, looks evil. Why do they go on shouting " Hosanna " ? Can they not see that this town is armed against such invocations ? It welcomes strangers with clamour and jangle, with shouts and execrations, with offensive smells. The air that rises from it is made dense with a cloud of harsh voices and of evil odours, thrusting themselves in betwixt town and sky, betwixt man and God.

" Alleluia !" The crowd grows even larger, and now many spread their garments in the way for his beast to tread on ; more and even more branches are strewed in his path ; children press close, and he has to pay heed less the ass should overturn any and set foot on them. " Hosanna !" If only this triumphal entry were over and done with ! Surely his own folk must be growing

uneasy ? Must it not surprise and disquiet
them that none of the wayfarers kneel ? These
onlookers are content to shout, to sing, and to
strew boughs, as if for a procession of mummers !

Suddenly he is awakened from his mood of
despondency and alarm, turned from his attitude
of passive defence. Hostile faces confront him ;
the procession is held up by a group of Pharisees ;
they have heard news of his arrival ; it is his
enemies who expect him, and recognise him when
he comes. Now they draw near—voices that
betray hatred even when uttering a welcome ;
faces in which pride peers from behind a mask of
humility. One of them says :

" Dost thou not hear what they are singing ?
Master, rebuke thy disciples !"

Then the prophet in him becomes dominant.
He faces them squarely, as he recalls everything
that has driven him hither ! Once more, he is
a fighter. Before coming to Jerusalem he has
known it to be a place where every one must
fight for his own hand, and he has come here to
conquer ! His answer is designed to force his
questioners to drop their pose of dispassionate-
ness, and, at the gate of the Holy City, he stresses
the conflict between his outlook and theirs. With
a loud voice, that all present may hear the words,
he says challengingly :

" I tell you that, if these should hold their
peace, the very stones would cry out !"

Abashed and angry, though taciturn as usual, the Pharisees depart. Again the rider is accompanied by the acclamations of the crowd. Then, above the uproar of the town, he hears a strident call. A trumpet sounds from the hilltop. That is a priest's summons.

Gazing at the hill, he urges on the ass, and takes the shortest way to the temple.

II.

Is this a market-place? Can the guide be making fools of them; showing them, to begin with, the centre of the profane world before taking them to the quiet sanctuary? Can this really be the house of the most High, this place of turmoil? A stern God, the ruler of the State, the Thinker, the vengeful Judge, may preside over these turbulent marble halls. It is no place for the kindly Father whose voice Jesus has heard in Galilee! When he had drawn near to the eastern, the main entrance, known as the Shushan Gate, and had been about to lay aside shoes and staff (having always understood this to be strictly enjoined by the law), he had been astonished to note that scarcely one of the thousands who were hurrying up the stairway had troubled to discard these tokens of worldly peregrination. "This is the court of the heathen," his thoughts ran. "Perhaps the throng is made up of un-

believers, come only to look on and not to pray."
Certainly, he hears many of them speak in
foreign tongues. On the walls, too, are notices
in three languages, warning the uncircumcised,
on pain of death, to venture no farther into the
temple. But most of the clamour is coming
from within, from the covered hall !

At length he stands in that inner hall, deafened
by the noise which rises in waves from all quarters
of the many-coloured pavement, and is re-echoed
from the cedarn roof. Sheep are to be seen by
twos and threes and in whole flocks as well ;
their bleating mingles with the cries of the men
squatting among them, the men who have brought
them for sale, each of whom tells the pilgrims
that his sheep are the fattest and the finest.
Buyers and sellers talk at the tops of their voices,
as they chaffer and gesticulate. Calves, too,
restlessly searching for their mothers, are lowing.
In one corner are the sellers of doves ; the birds
are tied together in pairs, by the legs, and flutter
their wings protestingly as the dealers hold them
aloft by the feet. The winesellers have flasks
of wine wrapped in straw, and there are sellers
of oil likewise ; they are all crying the price of
their wares. " Buy to-day, at a bargain ; to-
morrow you will have to pay more !" Many
other traffickers are there, offering sacks of grain,
bags of salt, and so on ; some of them so eager
that they seize a potential customer by the

ankles when he is about to pass unheeding.
Jesus is dumbfounded. This must be a night-
mare—a dream more strange than any he has
dreamed in Galilee.

Pushed forward by the surging crowd, separated
from his followers, alone amid the confusion,
Jesus now hears the clinking of coins upon
tables, the jingling of the bags that are shaken
by the money-changers who come here to
supply Jews from foreign parts with the local
money in which alone the temple dues can be
paid. For every half-siklus, they demand a full
sixth more than its normal exchange-value.
This is their licensed profit, in accordance with
the temple regulations, with the chartered right
conferred on them by the priests. Those among
the Jews who have nothing but outland money
demur and haggle. Now one of the money-
changers says he will be content with a seventh,
whereupon his neighbour cries out that this is
unfair, and threatens to inform the authorities.
All vie with one another in shouting, to the
perpetual accompaniment of clinking gold and
silver and copper. At these sights and these
sounds, Jesus of Nazareth is filled with wrath,
a righteous anger, fiercer than any he has known
before. The disturbing impressions of the last
day of the journey ; the uneasiness and the
mortification, the anger and the dread, the hope
and the disillusionment, of this hour of his entry

into the Holy City and his coming to the temple ;
the medley of feelings which have robbed him of
sleep and of appetite and even of the impetuosity
that had urged him southward from the tranquil
lakeside in Galilee—all these combine to call
forth the first terrible outbreak of his life.   In
his rage, he does not know himself ; any more
than he knows that this first outbreak is also to
be the last.

Clenching a fist that never before has been
clenched in anger, he thrusts it among the plates
and money-bags on the nearest table. Then,
as the coins fly hither and thither, he grips the
table with his left hand, and overturns it, so that
everything is scattered. Before the bystanders
have realised the situation, even before the
horrified money-changer, shouting his indigna-
tion, has gone down on all fours in a hasty attempt
to retrieve his possession, the infuriated prophet
is overthrowing the table of the next member of
the tribe. As a man who has never yet raised
his hand in wrath may, in some extremity, lay
about him sturdily like an angry giant, so does
this unarmed stranger now storm through the
hall of the temple, while all flee from him
affrighted. In a trice he is back among the
beasts brought hither for sacrifice. Snatching
a whip from one of the herdsmen, he lashes out
at animals and traders indiscriminately. As if
there were an earthquake, all flee panic-stricken

—dealers and foreigners ; the ungodly and the pious ; the lambs and the calves. They scurry helter-skelter down the stairway, to escape the thong of the scourge, while overhead fly some of the doves, winging their way to freedom. The menacing voice of Jesus rolls like thunder in the wake of the fugitives :

" It is written : ' My house shall be called the house of prayer ' ; but ye have made it a den of thieves."

The temple guards stand at gaze, without making any move to stop the expulsion. The first thoughts of the onlookers may be that Jesus is a man possessed. In a moment, superstition and hope, and, then, the memory of biblical texts, lead them to believe that what they are witnessing must be a revelation of the divine power in a human form. This must be a second Mattathias ; or perhaps Judas of Galilee, the zealot, has been reincarnated in a fellow country-man. He quoted the famous words of Jeremiah ! What do ordinary folk care about the losses of the traders and the money-changers, who make extortionate profits ? The guards would surely have intervened, had there been any wrong done. Their captain, evidently, feels that this man is filled with pious zeal, and that is why he gives no order for arrest. No one stirs to lay hands on the stranger, who is left alone in the great hall. Behind him are the huge pillars that line the corridor leading to the Holy of Holies. He sits down on one of the steps. The storm has passed. A man without influence, a man who has lived aloof from the world, he does not try to measure the significance or the scope of this victory won during his first hour in Jerusalem, or to think out a plan for safeguarding what he has gained and extending his conquest. He broods, exhausted and silent.

A number of children have stayed in the hall. Undismayed by his outburst, they have, rather, been diverted by the racket, and are now enjoying the freedom with which they can run to and fro in the cleared space. The boldest among them soon venture to approach the lonely figure. Thereupon his face softens into the smile he has ever ready for children and for women. He takes one of the youngsters on to his knees. Another of them had been among the spectators of the entry into Jerusalem, had heard the singing, and had joined his voice to the rest. This boy is quick to recognise the man who had been riding on the she-ass. Timidly at first, but with growing confidence, he begins to intone : " Hosanna to our King !" Soon the other lads join in, perhaps teasingly to begin with. Ere long there is a chorus of child voices singing : " Hosanna to our King !"

Now Jesus hears the call of his heart once more. The evil dream is suddenly dispelled.

With the passing of the storm in which, like
a Maccabean filled with the divine afflatus, he
has fought and won, he loses the power to renew
the effort.   In converse with these little children,
the teacher, the man of kindly feelings, is himself
once more.   Their king he may well be ; they
understand him, for theirs is the kingdom of
heaven.

Suddenly, fleeing like those whom he has
driven from this place, he goes forth, seeks and
finds some of his disciples, and hastens with them
away from the temple, to the Mount of Olives,
where there are friends to shelter him and care
for him, at Bethany.

III.

Next morning, however, an inner urge drives
him back to the city and the temple.   Has he,
during the night watches, questioned his Father ?
Has the sight of his disciples and his friends, have
the impressions aroused in his own mind by his
actions of yesterday (now that he has had time to
think them over quietly), strengthened him in his
purpose and summoned him to new deeds ?   His
mission steels him.   The sense of a high calling,
which has ever sustained this man, for all his
humility, spurs him on to the fight once more.
He has chosen a part out of scripture, and it
behoves him to play it to the end.   Perhaps his

enemies are too strong for him? Let them show
themselves so before the whole people !

They, meanwhile, had taken counsel together,
what time he, in silence, had sat at meat with
his friends. The first onslaught of the man whom
the Pharisees had lured hither, whose coming they
had so eagerly awaited, had been unexpectedly
successful. Yesterday, had he not supinely
drawn back when half way to his goal, he
could undoubtedly have become the leader o.
the people. For the populace was ever fickle,
as the history of the last thirty years had shown
again and again. God had guided the stranger's
footsteps away from the temple, and therefore the
law would be upheld ! To charge him with
a transgression on account of his actions of the
day before would be indiscreet, although it would
be easy enough to prove that the money-changers
and the dealers, with their coin and their live
stock, had every right to be in the temple. But
a man such as this Galilean, whose arrogance
was a danger to the priestly caste, must be
netted as an unbeliever, must be shown to have
infringed the prescripts of Holy Writ !

When he now returns to the temple, accompanied by two or three of his disciples, he keeps
away from the market place, and stays in the
western hall. His behaviour to-day is not that
of a zealot. He is a teacher, revered by many of
the people, decried by none, and extolled (more

or less openly) by many. When some of the scribes draw near, and, after a courteous greeting, seat themselves among the audience, making as if to begin a Talmudic disputation, the circle of hearers grows quickly, Now they will have a chance to learn whether the prophet of Galilee is able to do something more than, strong-handed, overturn tables and drive out beasts. The scribes ask one question after another, hiding their rancour to begin with. At length one of them enquires point-blank : " By what authority didst thou these things, and who gave thee this authority ?" Jesus may well have expected the question, for in this theocracy it was held that all power was from God, and the title to claim God's authority was not an easy one to establish. Being skilled in dialectics of the sort, he turned the question off by asking another :

" I also will ask you one thing, which if ye tell me, I in like wise will tell you by what authority I do these things. The baptism of John, whence was it, from heaven, or of men ?"

A silence followed, in which the scribes were turning the matter over within their minds. Their thoughts ran : " If we shall say, ' From heaven,' he will say unto us, ' Why did ye not then believe him ?' But if we shall say, ' Of men,' we fear the people, for all hold John to be a prophet." Prudence counselled evasion, so they made answer : " We cannot tell."

With a quizzical smile, Jesus turns from them, saying : " Neither tell I you by what authority I do these things !"

The audience nod approvingly, for the common folk are always amused by such a duel of wits in which one party is nonplussed.   Half the town will know this evening how the scribes have been put out of countenance by the prophet from Galilee.   He is in the vein now.   Yesterday he made a mistake by failing (for lack of bodily strength) to follow up the victory he had won in the world of matter.   Now he makes a mistake of the reverse kind, by following up the victory he has won in the world of the spirit.   Has he decided to inflict a public defeat on his enemies ? Or is it merely a point of pride with him, in Jerusalem and in the temple, to bring into play the very last reserves of his fighting forces ? Whatever the motive, he propounds to his adversaries a parable.   A man had two sons.   To one of them the father said : " Son, go work to-day in my vineyard."   The young man refused to go, but afterwards repented and went.   The other son, when likewise told to work in the vineyard, promised to go, and did not.   " Which of the twain did the will of his father ?"

" The former," answer the scribes in the hope that their reply will provoke an insulting rejoinder. They have their wish, for Jesus assumes the offensive.   Showing strong emotion, he speaks in

16

a loud tone : " Verily I say unto you that the
publicans and the harlots go into the kingdom of
God before you.   John came, and taught you the
way of righteousness, and ye believed him not ;
but the publicans and the harlots believed
him."

The people listen with mingled alarm and
veneration. Do not this teacher's words recall
John's ? Those whose aim it is to destroy him
are at once enraged and delighted, for, when he
thus openly insults them, he is committing himself
more and more hopelessly, and soon they will
have him in their snare. For his part, while
he is deliberately attacking them, he is ignorant
of his own danger. Unacquainted with the
artifices of Jerusalem, when he has delivered
this thrust he once more brandishes his spiritual
weapon, heaping parable upon parable in such
a way as to forfeit his advantage. For what he
now says of the householder and the vineyard
is confused. He mixes his metaphors, and
becomes personal. Of a sudden he breaks into
menace : " The kingdom of God shall be taken
from you, and given to the heathen, who will
bring forth the fruits thereof !"

His hearers are staggered. The saying is too
hard for them, and they cannot stomach it.
The scribes find the soil prepared, when they go
from one to another and whisper that Jesus must
surely be deranged. The sail of popular favour,

which in the calm of the last half-hour has been
hanging slackly, is blown over upon a new tack.
The men who hold power and wield influence
now find it easy, through their tools, to work
upon popular opinion. When the money-
changers come back to their tables, when the
traffic without which the pilgrims from afar
cannot sacrifice at the Passover is resumed,
people begin to smile and then to laugh out loud
at the crazy Galilean, who was yesterday so
zealous to uproot established customs, and who
now looks on indifferently when the old practices
are resumed, content to sit upon the steps in
crack-jaw disputation with the men of learning.

He is sensitive to the change in mood, which
can be read in all men's faces. Discouraged
after his partial victory, he realises that this
uncongenial atmosphere, this city with its agelong
laws and traditions, is capable of breaking the
strongest spirit. Once more, sad and yet defiant,
he escapes from the prison of its walls, to seek his
quiet place of refuge in the outskirts.

He is athirst, for he has been talking most of
the forenoon, and the heat of the day has begun.
He will not seek the streets where fruitsellers are
to be found ; here, on the western slopes of the
Mount of Olives, there must be plenty of fruit
to be had for the plucking. So much, during
these two days, has his mind been distracted from
the happenings of ordinary life, that he forgets

the season of the year, forgets that Passover is
still to come, and looks for figs on a tree that has
but recently burst into leaf. In his homeland he
had often noted the due succession of flower and
fruit, and would never have dreamed of expecting
to find figs till June. Yet here, in arid Judea,
he looks for them before April has drawn to a
close. Since the froward tree has no figs ready
for his eating, and since his thirst is intensified by
disappointment, he raises his hand and curses
it, saying :

" Let no man eat fruit of thee hereafter for
ever !"

During the time of his mission, a year and more,
Jesus has uttered many blessings, though never
a curse. Of late, he has given vent to threats
and warnings, but not to maledictions. In the
temple, that morning, he had gone so far as to
utter a grim prophecy excluding the hypocritical
scribes and Pharisees from the kingdom of heaven.
Now, on the baking hillside, when he is tired and
thirsty, out of humour after his controversy with
his enemies, he finds a target for his wrath in the
innocent tree, which bears naught but leaves and
flowers at this season, as God has ordained. He
ignores his talent for blessing, and summons all
the powers which he believes himself possessed
of as Son of God in order to blast one of the
harmless creatures of God the Father.

Thus does the sun of Jerusalem gnaw like

a canker at the heart of a prophet who, in the simpler world of Galilee, had never swerved from his path.

IV.

The Pharisees and the Sadducees have put their heads together, for, though sundered by veiled enmity, they are united by their dread of the common foe. The stranger seems to them a greater menace than either he or his disciples imagine. The magnates of the Holy City are better acquainted than is the Galilean with the levity of Jerusalem, with the fickleness of the crowd, with people's readiness to run after any new thing, with the growth of faction, with the lack of respect for authority. The priests, in frequent receipt of messages from many lands warning them of the imminence of a dissolution of the existing order, and telling of new sects and fresh interpretations of prophecy, may well be assured, when they contemplate the temper of the multitude, that an energetic man armed with a few telling catchwords could easily sow disorder in this festal crowd, perhaps initiate a serious rising.

True, the prophet hardly seems to be a man of action ; he is not full of ardour, as was John ; nevertheless, he knows how to quote scripture against the priests. He may be right in much

that he says, though such words as his cannot
be tolerated for public consumption. The
triumphal entry into the town was probably
not so much his own doing as the outcome of
the excessive enthusiasm of his disciples, and it
is likely enough that he has already forgotten his
outburst of yesterday against the money-changers
in the temple. But to cry aloud in the outer
court that publicans, harlots, and the heathen
will enter the kingdom of heaven before the
elect among the Jews! Such teaching contains
the seed of grave dangers. The man who utters
it must be silenced!

" If we could but know," think the Pharisees,
" what these easy-going Sadducees really have
it in their minds to do! Are they only making
pretence of helping us, while really determined
to remain passive, as usual? What about setting
the Herodians to work?" Then the abyss would
be spanned. For the adherents of the house
of Herod, those of Herod Antipas in existing
circumstances, have, since the break-up of the
Herodian realm, been waiting for a chance to
re-establish it. In the bottom of their hearts,
therefore, they are hostile to the Romans; are
likewise hostile to any Messiah sprung from the
people. The Sadducees are friendly to the
Romans, but hostile to a Messiah. By joining
hands with these two extremes a bridge could be
built. Perhaps a political query would suffice

to trip up this simple-minded prophet. If, in answer to it, he were to say anything against Rome, the governor would have him arrested, and he would be tried for a political offence. Were he to proclaim himself the Messiah, the Herodians would also take action, and they are full of confidence to-day, seeing that Herod Antipas is here, having arrived yesterday to celebrate the Passover in Jerusalem. There must, of course, be nothing spectacular, nothing that would attract too large a concourse of onlookers.

Quite unconcernedly, therefore, as if no more were afoot than a debate about Holy Writ, next day in the temple a couple of young fellows who have been well primed by the Pharisees and the Herodians, accost the stranger from Galilee. One of them says to him civilly :

" Master, we know that thou art true, and teachest the way of God in truth, neither carest thou for any man, for thou regardest not the person of men.   Tell us, therefore, what thinkest thou ; is it lawful to give tribute unto Cæsar, or not?"

Jesus has never troubled himself about the question of taxation, or about the emperor. If, once, in Capernaum, he had demurred to the payment of tribute, it was only in a passing moment of spiritual pride, when he wished to assert himself as a king's son, before paying.

Now, however, he thinks of his fellow country-
man, Judas of Galilee, who had led a revolt
against the payment of taxes to the Romans.
Judas had regarded such a sign of subserviency
as shameful, and had appealed to the nation
to throw off the yoke of its oppressors. In early
boyhood this tale had stirred Jesus profoundly ;
now it seems to him that the matter has nothing
to do with his new kingdom. He sees the trap
underlying the question, and is not concerned
to hide his knowledge, so he answers :

" Why tempt ye me, ye hypocrites ? Show
me the tribute money."

Thereupon they show him a Roman penny,
which one of them has brought, to spur on Jesus
the more with a sight of the forbidden image.
He is content to ask :

" Whose image is this, and whose name is
inscribed upon the coin ?"

" Cæsar's."

" Render, therefore, unto Cæsar the things
that are Cæsar's ; and unto God the things that
are God's."

By this masterly rejoinder they are silenced
and discountenanced, feeling themselves detected,
chidden, and defeated.

When word of this is brought to the Sadducees,
they cannot avoid a chuckle at the reverse
sustained by their adversaries ; still, they think
it well to take the field on their own account, in

order to make Jesus look ridiculous. Has he not
spoken of the resurrection of the dead, in which the
Pharisees likewise believe? For their part, they
think that death ends all. Some of them,
therefore, accosting him in the temple, pose a
quaint problem. A woman has married seven
brothers in succession, and has had no child
by any of them. Then the woman dies, and
meets her husbands in heaven. In this life she
had been wife to them all : whose wife shall she
be after the resurrection? The Sadducees, surrounded by the crowd that always flocks to attend
a biblical discussion in the temple, await an
answer. How can he fail to give one that will
seem absurd? No matter to which of the seven
husbands he may allot the wife, the other six will
be disappointed. Jesus has an answer which is
not ridiculous :

"Ye do err, not knowing the scriptures, nor
the power of God. For in the resurrection they
neither marry, nor are given in marriage, but
are as the angels of God in heaven. As touching
the resurrection of the dead, have ye not read
that which was spoken to you by God, saying :
'I am the God of Abraham, and the God of
Isaac, and the God of Jacob'? God is not the
God of the dead, but of the living."

The learned among his audience are astonished.
Many of them realise how deeply this layman has
fathomed the spirit of Holy Writ ; yet they hold

their peace. But the Pharisees are full of glee
because Jesus has worsted their enemies the
Sadducees. It seems as if the two factions were
to go on vying each with the other in the
endeavour to bring Jesus to confusion. The
Pharisees' turn having come, they send one man,
a scribe, who asks :

" Master, which is the greatest of all the
commandments ?"

Jesus answers :

" It is this, ' Hear, O Israel, the Lord our God
is one God, and thou shalt love the Lord thy God
with all thy heart, and with all thy soul, and with
all thy mind, and with all thy strength.' But
there is a second, which is no less great, ' Thou
shalt love thy neighbour as thyself.' There is no
greater commandment than this."

The word strikes home. The questioner feels
obscurely that old doctrine and new interpretation lie here side by side in two sentences.
Forgetting his errand, he nods approvingly, and
rejoins : " Master, thou hast said the truth."
Then he repeats Jesus' words, and adds : " That
is more than all burnt offerings and sacrifices."

Jesus, hearing the quiet admission, is prompt
to meet it in a friendly spirit, and replies :

" Thou art not far from the kingdom of God."

Thus, for a moment, the two worlds understand one another.

" Is it impossible to catch him napping ?"

wonder the Pharisees, when their emissary comes
to report.   What if he could be snared by an
appeal to that very kindness of heart which
inclines him to be so gentle to sinners ?   One of
their number has news that during the previous
night a woman was taken in adultery.   The town
is buzzing with the tale.   What if she were led
before the prophet, and he were to declare she
ought to be set at liberty ?

Sending for the prisoner, they seek out Jesus,
and find him with his disciples, seated on the
sand in one of the outer courts, at the foot of the
fourteen steps that lead to the interior of the
temple.   He looks up in astonishment at the
size of the crowd which has hunted him out—
for many have pressed after, seeing a woman
haled through the streets.

" Who is this woman ?" says his questioning
glance.   He looks at her attentively.

" Master," says one of those who hold her,
" this woman was taken in adultery, in the very
act.   Now Moses in the law commanded us,
that such should be stoned : but what sayest
thou ?"

Jesus has looked more closely at the woman
than at her accuser.   The latter seems to him
filled with rancorous zeal, whilst the culprit
is overwhelmed with grief and shame. Shall
he answer the question in accordance with the
promptings of his heart ?   Is there any one here

who will understand him if he does? When all
eyes are fixed on him, he lowers his own, looks
at the sand, stoops, and begins to write in it
with his finger. The bystanders regard him in
silence for a while, wonderingly. Then, once
more, the original questioner asks him for his
opinion. He raises his eyes, and (since he cannot
attempt to defend the sinner, yet loves penitence, while hating the ostentatious purity which
plumes itself and is ever ready to condemn) says
gently in words that go straight to the heart of
the accuser :

" He that is without sin among you, let him
cast the first stone !"

Once more he stoops, as if himself ashamed,
and goes on writing in the sand.

Never in his life did his words have a more
powerful influence than now.

In Galilee, many had been brought to
repentance by his utterances. Publicans had
abandoned their sinful occupation. A harlot
had wept, contrite at the sight of his unfeigned
humility, and had learned from him a new kind
of love. That very morning, one of the scribes had
been constrained to admit the truth of his words.
Now this gentle saying moves and softens the
arrogant and self-righteous persons who had seized
the adulteress and had been eager for her death.
Each of them feels a conviction of sin, of sin un-
atoned. Not one of them has strength to cast a

stone at her. Suddenly they loose the woman, and silently disperse as if fain to hide from one another. The prophet is left alone with the sinner.

Jesus stands up and asks a question. In doing so, he gives the answer; for he makes a sweeping gesture at the vacant space whence all have noiselessly departed, aware of their own guilt.

"Woman, where are thy accusers? Hath no man condemned thee?"

In the voice of one redeemed, she answers:

"No man, Lord."

Faced by the sinner, he forgets his new rôle. The overweening self-confidence of the Messiah vanishes for the nonce. Conscious that he, like all the others, is but a man, he says to her, with a hidden meaning:

"Neither do I condemn thee. Go and sin no more."

V.

Or was it that he doubted himself? Could it be that the parching atmosphere of Jerusalem was already drying up the springs of his imagination? Three days had gone by, and nothing had happened beyond some trifling disputes about words, customs, matters of no moment. What wonders had he worked? Where was the stream of faith which he had hoped to bring

forth from this arid rock, smiting it like Moses
in Horeb ? According to his disciples there was
a slight movement of interest among the people,
some being for him and some against ; yet, what
of the festival and the general influx of strangers,
what of a hundred novelties, the driving out of the
money-changers was wellnigh forgotten. Since
there had been no further incident to stimulate
faith or even to arouse curiosity, both hope and
fear were dying, and the goal seemed more
distant day by day.

Now, for the fourth time on his way to the
temple, he has made up his mind that he will
himself propound a question, in order to find out
what people think of his mission, whether any one
believes in it outside the circle of his own immediate followers. In front of the grotto of Pan
near Cæsarea Philippi, an uneasy feeling had
prompted him to ask the disciples for whom they
took him. Now, in the hall where the Pharisees
have learned to expect his coming every forenoon,
a like feeling (in which dread is to-day pre-
dominant) leads him to turn the conversation to
the topic of the Messiah. He speaks in veiled
terms. Since he has to deal this time, not with
enthusiastic young disciples, but with elderly
scribes, he puts his question as if it concerned
a point of interpretation, asking :

" What think ye of Christ ? Whose son is he ?"

" The son of David," reply the Pharisees.

" How, then, doth David in spirit call him
' Lord,' saying : ' The Lord said unto my Lord,
" Sit thou on my right hand, till I make thine
enemies my footstool " '?   If David then call him
' Lord,' how is he his son ?"

The question remains unanswered.   But shrewd
members of the audience (and all the Pharisees
are shrewd) are quick to infer that Jesus is a man
who feels that he is perhaps the Messiah, and
recognises that his Galilean birth, and his origin
from a stock which does not spring from the house
of David, are stumbling-blocks in his path.   He
is trying to twist the meaning of the ancient
texts ; to forestall objections.   " This shows,"
think the Pharisees, blinking as they sit round him
in a circle, " that conviction is strong within
him, that he has little doubt now of being the
Christ."

Receiving no answer to his enquiry, contemplating these shrewd men as they silently
encompass him, accustomed to watch his auditors
and to read people's minds from their faces,
seeing now that there is no responsive sympathy
in the eyes of the multitude, wearied by the
thrust and parry of thought against thought and
phrase against phrase, overstrained by the fruitless endeavour to find a way out—he makes a last
desperate effort.   Since his enemies' onslaught
appears to have been stayed, he will himself take
the offensive.

Somewhere in the temple, a moment must have
come when the multitude gathered round him,
clamouring for a sermon, as so often at home in
Galilee. Collecting his forces, he uttered in plain
words all that he had been wont to think of the
Pharisees. Here in the temple, before his star
had paled, he would deliver his mind. These
self-righteous burghers who had always been his
most deadly foes should hear plain truth for once.
He, Jesus, would dare to utter it ; and if in his
words they could find a means whereby to lay
him low—then, so much the better !

" The scribes and the Pharisees sit in Moses'
seat." Thus he begins, without directly coun-
selling revolt. " All, therefore, whatsoever they
bid you observe, that observe and do : but do not
ye after their works ; for they say, and do not !
They bind heavy burdens and grievous to be
borne, and lay them on men's shoulders ; but they
themselves will not move them with one of their
fingers. All their works they do for to be seen
of men : they make broad their phylacteries, and
enlarge the borders of their garments, and love
the uppermost rooms at feasts, and the chief seats
in the synagogues, and greetings in the markets,
and to be called of men ' Rabbi, Rabbi.' . . .
Woe unto you, scribes and Pharisees, hypocrites ;
for ye shut up the kingdom of heaven against
men. Ye neither go in yourselves, nor suffer
ye them that are entering to go in ! . . .

"Ye say : 'Whosoever shall swear by the temple, it is nothing ; but whosoever shall swear by the gold of the temple, he is a debtor.' Ye fools and blind : for which is greater, the gold, or the temple that sanctifieth the gold ? . . . Ye hypocrites ! Ye pay tithe of mint and anise and cummin, and have omitted the weightier matters of the law ; judgment, mercy, and faith : these ought ye to have done, and not to leave the other undone. . . . Ye strain at a gnat, and swallow a camel. . . . Ye make clean the outside of the cup and of the platter, but within they are full of extortion and excess. Thou blind Pharisee, cleanse first that which is within the cup and the platter, that the outside of them may be clean also ! . . . Ye are like unto whited sepulchres, which indeed appear beautiful out-ward, but are within full of dead men's bones, and of all uncleanness ! Even so ye also outwardly appear righteous unto men, but within ye are full of hypocrisy and iniquity ! . . . Ye build the tombs of the prophets, . . . and say : ' If we had been in the days of our fathers, we would not have been partakers with them in the blood of the prophets.' . . . Fill ye up then the measure of your fathers ! Ye serpents, ye viper's brood, how shall ye escape the damnation of hell ?"

The horrified hearers feel that John must have risen from the dead ! Must it not give him pause to find that, at the close of a career upon whose

17

threshold that prophet had stood as a sign, he has himself lapsed into the crude invectives which he had found so distasteful in the Baptist? Never again! Away from this temple, where true piety is unknown, and where only its caricature stalks triumphant. As he hastily seeks an exit, pushing his way through the crowd, followed by his disciples, in the next court he sees people thronging round the thirteen chests which the treasurer of the temple has placed side by side, to receive the oblations of the faithful.

Here he catches sight of a poor old woman who is laboriously extracting some coins from the folds of a cloth in which she has wrapped them, and is looking for the slit through which her money is to be dropped. Elbowed aside by the well-to-do, who on feast days are wont to come in great numbers and ostentatiously to cast in large sums, she stands there tremulous and abashed. At length, with clumsy fingers, she manages to throw in two mites—the smallest of copper coins. Jesus is greatly moved, now that, at long last, he sees sterling piety in Jerusalem. He turns to the disciples, saying :

"Verily this poor widow hath cast more in than all the others who have cast into the treasury. For they gave of their abundance. But she, in her poverty, cast in all that she had."

VI.

The disciples do not understand him : neither the disaster which threatens him ; nor the doubts which oppress him.   They do not even grasp the nature of the disappointment which these days in Jerusalem have brought him.   All they had wanted was to become centres of public attention.   If they now made any special appeal to him, it was not concerning matters belonging to the kingdom of heaven.   Thus, one day, Salome, mother of James and John, came to him, followed by her two sons, so that it was plain they had moved her to what she did.   The three knelt before him, and Salome said : " Master, grant that my two sons may sit, the one on thy right hand, and the other on the left, in thy kingdom."

Such, then, were the requests of his favourite disciples !   Had they spent a year and longer in close companionship with him, to learn in the end no more from his teaching than this ?   For them the kingdom of heaven was a place into which they would transport, above the clouds, an ambition which might be seemly enough in the children of this world !   With mingled feelings of pride and anger, he rejoined :

" Ye know not what ye ask.   Are ye able to drink of the cup that I shall drink of ?"   When

they had answered " We are able," he went on
in a kindlier tone : " To sit on my right hand,
and on my left, is not mine to give, but my
Father's."

Next day he is disturbed in his musings by the
noise of strife among them.   They are wrangling
as to which of them is to be accounted the
greatest.   Throughout the time of his mission,
he has taught them that none of them is to set
himself above the others ; that in the new kingdom there is to be no place of authority or power,
there are to be no gradations of precedence.   Now
they are at odds one with another about this
very question of supremacy !   Intervening, he
says bitterly :

" The kings of this world hold sway in the world,
and they that rule there are called gracious lords.
But ye shall not be so !   He that is greatest among
you, let him be as the younger ; and he that is
chief, as he that doth serve.   For who is greater,
he that sitteth at meat, or he that serveth ?   Is
it not he that sitteth at meat ?   But I am among
you as he that serveth."

When the disciples were disputing in such
fashion, and also about what the Master had
better do and leave undone during these days in
Jerusalem, one among them was a silent auditor.
Judas now seemed more inclined to think than
to talk.

The only one of these men and women who was

not of Galilean origin, he had, a good while back, quitted Judea. At first, perhaps, he had designed to follow John rather than Jesus, for the Baptist's teaching may well have been more congenial to him than that of the Nazarene. He would seem to have broken away from his own folk, to have abandoned a handicraft, to have forsaken money and possessions—for he was a man of practical bent, and was therefore made the keeper of the common purse. He alone among the disciples had known something of the great world before joining the fellowship of the prophet who had neither part nor lot in the things of this world. He knew the ways of the authorities, and he knew Jerusalem. He knew all that he had renounced, and why. Those who now became his brethren were youthful enthusiasts, brought up in narrow surroundings. Endowed with the heedlessness, the restless instability, of the Galilean temperament, they had impetuously left the plough, or cast aside nets and fish-hooks, as soon as the gentle message of the carpenter's son assailed their ears.

Whatever his new Master did, Judas would turn over and over lovingly in his mind, wondering what he himself would have done in Jesus' place, and whether Jesus had acted for the best. Now, when the company had come southward into Judas' homeland, the associations of youth were revived. With the revival of memories

of kin and handicraft, with the recurrence of the
thoughts and feelings that had driven him from
Judea, his uneasiness grew—a disquiet as great,
perhaps, as Jesus' own. What was happening?
What was the Master doing to ensure the attainment of the goal, to ensure the attainment of
power? Did he really believe that God would
thrust a hand down into the confusions of this
world, in order to smooth his Son's path? Day
after day the disciple was on the tiptoe of expectation, as he stood with the others in the temple,
listening to the parables, watching the thrust
and parry of the disputations. But there was no
sign of progress. Nothing had been gained since,
on the opening day, the prophet had, with heroic
gesture, driven out his foes. The hero dwindled,
neglecting to follow up his advantage.

Meanwhile Judas' relatives and former asso-
ciates in Jerusalem were whispering at the
dissatisfied follower's ear, intensifying his doubts.
This, then, was his Master? For this he had
thrown up a solid position, had left his goods
behind, to walk in the footsteps of a crazy fanatic
who had not even the mother-wit needed for
a prophet's calling? After his long absence,
the Judean saw a renewed charm in the pomp
of priesthood, the splendour of vestments, the
imposing array of public ceremonial. But the
man for whose sake he had abandoned all these
things had ridden into Jerusalem seated on

a she-ass, humble of mien, and now remained
inert.

Thus did Judas listen with steadily growing
doubt to every word of his Master, faithfully
determined to decide justly, not jumping to an
unfair conclusion. The more Jesus obscured his
thoughts from his followers, the more uneasy
did this disciple become, for it seemed to Judas
that his leader was squandering the last hours
in which effective action was still possible. To
him, with his experience of city life, it was plainer
than it was to the others that, behind the scenes,
the powers of the law were being concentrated
to crush the troublesome visionary. He was the
first to guess that the last speech in the temple,
with which the discouraged prophet had alarmed
rather than enlightened his disciples, was the
outcome of a presage of imminent death.

Now Jesus seems to collect his forces again.
With all the might of his faith he once more
displays himself to his followers as the Messiah.
Amid the tribulations he prophesies, the famines
and the earthquakes, he presents himself as the
saviour. It is over the supper-table at Bethany,
on the fifth evening, that he speaks as follows to
the circle of his intimates :

" And then shall all the tribes of the earth
mourn, and they shall see the Son of Man coming
in the clouds of heaven with power and glory.
And he shall send his angels with a great sound

of a trumpet, and they shall gather together his elect from the four winds, from one end of heaven to the other. . . . This generation shall not pass till all these things are fulfilled. Heaven and earth shall pass away, but my words shall not pass away. . . . When the Son of Man shall come in his glory, and all the holy angels with him, then shall he sit upon the throne of his glory. And before him shall be gathered all nations : and he shall separate them one from another, as a shepherd divideth his sheep from his goats ; and he shall set the sheep on his right hand, but the goats on his left. Then shall the King say unto them on his right hand : Come, ye blessed of my Father, inherit the kingdom prepared for you from the foundation of the world. For I was hungry, and ye gave me meat ; I was thirsty, and ye gave me drink. . . . Inasmuch as ye have done it unto the least of these my brethren, ye have done it unto me !''

In this wise does he allot salvation and damnation to those who have done good and to those who have done evil, depicting himself (more emphatically than ever before) as heavenly judge, and not hesitating to announce that those who now hear his words will, while still in the flesh, see him descending from the skies. Since Jerusalem will not listen to his message, he conveys it in these terms to the little group of the faithful, and holds fast to the thoughts conceived

at Cæsarea Philippi. Sitting in a circle round
him, they gaze at him and believe. One only
finds it hard to accept these utterances. Why
should this man, who has day after day failed
to maintain his ground in public, thus vaunt his
power and his glory in private? Judas' doubts
are intensified.

When silence at length broods over the table,
those assembled there are joined by a woman
who during these days has learned to know the
stranger staying with her friends, and has come
to regard him with veneration. She bears in her
hands an alabaster flask filled with spikenard,
a precious Indian perfume, which ordinarily
is used only drop by drop. Breaking the neck
of the flask, she pours the whole of the contents
over the hair of the man who has brought her
to the faith. All present contemplate this costly
anointing in an amazed silence. All, with one
exception. Judas, in whom doubt is coming to
a crisis, ventures to blame even the Master,
for failing to check such prodigality. He exclaims :

" Why was not this oil sold? It is worth
three hundred pence, which might have been
given to the poor !"

For Jesus, this censure from one of his followers
is a new experience. He looks steadfastly at the
man whose voice has been raised against him. Is
revolt beginning in his own household? Perhaps

Judas is merely speaking in haste, urged on by the parsimonious calculation that money which might have gone to swell the contents of the joint purse has been wasted on the Master's hair ? In a tone of gentle reproof, Jesus says :

" Let her alone. Why trouble ye her ? She has wrought a good work on me. For ye have the poor with you always, and whensoever ye will ye may do them good : but me ye have not always. She hath done what she could : she is come aforehand to anoint my body for the burying."

Amid the gloomy thoughts aroused by his own words, he is silent for a space. Then, more gracious than ever to the woman who has anointed him, he says, in the tone of the prophets of old :

" Wheresoever this gospel shall be preached throughout the whole world, this also that she has done shall be spoken of for a memorial of her."

VII.

Judas was in a bitter mood. He had devoted all his energies to gaining funds for the benefit of the poor. He had sacrificed his worldly possessions that he might give himself up to the cultivation of the inner life. Now he was at a

loose end. It seemed to him that he had been
cheated by behaviour which had squandered
three hundred pence in an aromatic salutation,
in an act of extravagant homage. Doubt bit into
his heart like a flame. In view of his Master's
growing inertia, he may well have recalled the
vivid saying of Moses : " When a prophet
speaketh in the name of the Lord, if the thing
follow not, nor come to pass, that is the thing
which the Lord hath not spoken, but the prophet
hath spoken it presumptuously : thou shalt not
be afraid of him." The warnings and the
mockery of his relatives and of his old friends in
Jerusalem, renewed day by day, gathered force
in his mind. He no longer resisted the influence
of early associations. Since his Master remained
passive, he would himself take action. Why
should he not put an end to the intolerable
oppressions of this period of waiting ?

Turn away, and forsake the Master ? This
would be too little, and too much. He wanted
to force both Jesus and the enemies of Jesus to
take a decisive step. In search of a worthy
motive, trying to find in apostolic zeal a justifica-
tion for what was in truth the personal animus
of disappointed ambition, he discovered what he
wanted in a new train of thought. Had not the
Master again and again of late, in ever new
phraseology, described his expected sufferings
as stages on the road to glory ? Had he not

actually spoken of his death as imminent? If
he were really the Messiah, and refrained from
proving this by his actions, he could only establish his claim to the title by passion, by suffering
before the eyes of men. Jesus' antagonism to
the temple and its official representatives was
plain from the arguments, the invectives, and the
complaints of both parties. If he were now
delivered into the grasp of his enemies, the essential truth of his gospel would be made plain to
all the world.

The disciple who was instrumental in rushing
the Master into the way of suffering, and this
disciple alone, would therefore open to him the
path of glory. Perhaps Jesus, in his sublime
resignation, was only waiting for the helper who
would bring him to the end, and thus to the
beginning? If God were to work a miracle,
so that his Son should at the last prove victorious,
the apparently faithless disciple would be doubly
justified. Jesus would have given proof of divine
power both to himself and to his follower.
Doubt in the genuineness of his mission would
have been dispelled for ever.

Such were the thoughts with which Judas tried
to cover up his own weakness, to mollify his
vexation with himself for having had faith in
Jesus, and his still greater vexation because that
faith had now grown cold. Such were the
thoughts with which his mind was filled when he

was on his way to the house of a leading member of the priesthood—a place well known to him during his earlier days in Jerusalem.

The door was closed swiftly behind him when he entered. Some members of the Great Council were assembled here to discuss the situation. Prompt action was essential. It was but two days more to the feast of the Passover. If this Nazarene were then, before the assembled crowds, to utter another diatribe against those who sat in Moses' seat, there would be grave danger. His arrest must be effected quietly, far away from the temple and from other places of public resort. He must be condemned and executed before the festival, upon the evidence of two or three witnesses who would now be forthcoming. Then the ferment would speedily subside.

The leaders knew all this. They knew also that it might be dangerous to send a company of armed men to Bethany, to surround the quiet house, and to seize a number of persons who would perhaps resist arrest. This might well provoke a riot. Here, however, was one of the man's own disciples willing to take a hand in the game. In that case it would be enough to notify the supreme authority, and the whole matter could be dealt with that very evening. Judas, it seems, must have been told not to let his Master out of his eyes.

Jesus, wishing to fulfil the duty of every pious

Jew on the festal Thursday, had ordered a paschal lamb in the city. Though he was wont to speak slightingly of sacrificial observances, he clung to this ancient custom. Moreover, he may well have been influenced by a desire to eat the paschal lamb for the first and doubtless the last time in the very town of Jerusalem. As was the custom here, the guests were given a room to themselves, with cushions and coverlets. They brought their own meat and wine, and left the skin of the lamb for their host as a thank-offering. The leaven was removed from the house. In memory of the afflictions in Egypt, there were prepared a thin cake or biscuit made of wheaten meal, and a thick stew of fruit with bitter herbs. The disciples, having bought the lamb, took it to the temple, waiting their turn among thousands for the blessing; and finally they joined in the throng of those making their way to the priestly slaughterers. These sang psalms as they did their holy work, regardless of the mess of blood and entrails, the bleatings of the beasts, and the trumpet-blasts of the servitors of the temple.

Coming down into the city that evening, Jesus found the room prepared. Four huge cushions, all with coverlets, had been arranged in a half-circle. On each of them, three persons could recline. Only the twelve had come—no women. Jesus had the place of honour in the middle, flanked by two chosen disciples, Peter and John. He was careful to observe all the ceremonies proper to the occasion, but gave to each a peculiar significance, in order to show that the end was drawing near.

As they took their places, he said : " With desire I have desired to eat this Passover with you before I suffer. For I say unto you, I will not any more eat thereof, until everything has been fulfilled in the kingdom of God." Then they brought him red wine, which he mixed with water, and blessed the first cup : " Praise be unto thee, O Lord our God, King of the world, who hast created the fruit of the vine." When the cup had gone the round, he added : " I will not drink henceforth of this fruit of the vine until the kingdom of heaven shall come."

Not until now was the table brought in. It was so low that they could eat from it lying down : first the bitter herbs, and afterwards the stew of fruit, giving thanks to God for each. The table was removed, before the second cup was mixed. The wine went round the circle to the accompaniment of song. Then the table was brought in again. On it two flat loaves of bread were lying : Jesus broke fragments from one of them and laid them upon the loaf whence they had been broken, saying : " Blessed be he who brings bread out of the earth !" He wrapped a morsel of the bread in some of the herbs, dipped it in the fruit stew, ate it, and offered up another prayer. Not until then was the lamb brought in. Thereupon, all mingling their fingers in the dish after the oriental fashion, they began their meal.

For a space one looking on from a distance might fancy that here was nothing more than an assembly of cheerful folk, consuming God's gifts reverently and thankfully. Indeed, Jesus is eating with his disciples much as usual, but in mind he is aloof from them. He feels that his battle has been lost, that his mission is a failure, and that he is lonely though among friends. Are they really his friends ? Which of them is still to be trusted ? Does any one of them understand him ? Would the twelve, men of peace not of war, fight for him ; would they even say a word on his behalf? They have always been weaklings. Now, within a few days, since coming to this unfriendly town, their faith has grown cold. Not one of them is man enough to carry on a struggle which even the Master has abandoned.

Is he thinking of them all, as these doubts course through his mind ? Does he distrust all of those who dip their hands in the dish ? Or does he, with a seer's vision, raise his eyes from the hand to the face of Judas, whose fingers are made tremulous by the conflict which rages within ? However this may be, Jesus, suddenly withdrawing his own hand from the dish, exclaims :

" One of you who eat with me shall betray me."

They are all horror-stricken. Every hand is withdrawn from the dish. They look at one another ; they look at Jesus ; they look at one another again. What has happened ? Is it possible that, having a premonition of impending disaster, he guesses that not one of the disciples is really a stalwart supporter, that in their hearts all twelve of them are potential traitors ? Does he know that one of the two lying cheek by jowl with him will deny him that very night, with a denial tantamount to treason ? Or, with his shrewd judgment of character, has he grasped the import of Judas' silent scrutiny ; does he know that this man is his secret foe ?

In Judas, at any rate, the shaft strikes home, for alone of them all he knows what the Master means. Were Jesus now to stand up and point to him with accusing finger, saying, " Thou art the man. Thou hast it in mind to betray me," he could convert a sinner—and find more joy in this repentant one than in the eleven righteous apostles who will in the end forsake him. This is the moment in which Judas the doubter, Judas the disappointed, would pay homage to the royal might of the Son of God. As if the lightning of heaven had sought him out, he would sink at Jesus' feet, and would pray to the Master whom he had wronged ! Does not Jesus see how pale

18

is the traitor, aware of his guilt ? Do none of the others notice how Judas' hand is shaking, and how he tries to keep his face in shadow ?

" Is it I ?"—" Is it I ?"—asks one of the disciples after another, thus manifesting, like little children, their humility and their confidence in his words. Even Judas parrots the phrase, waiting for the flash of anger in Jesus' eyes. But Jesus is content to say :

" It is one of the twelve, that dippeth with me in the dish. The Son of Man indeed goeth, as it is written of him : but woe to that man by whom the Son of Man is betrayed ! Good were it for that man if he had never been born !"

" No more than this ?" thinks Judas, his tension relaxing. Only the will to die ? Not so much energy, even, as to denounce him to the others ? And this is the prophet on whose strength we have been building ! He does not know which of us will betray him ; or, if he knows, he will succumb without a struggle ! Here is a riddle which death alone can solve !

The meal dragged on gloomily, for the springs of conversation had been choked. Talk of betrayal had come as the seal to the other warnings of the nearness of the end. Again and again, that evening, had the Master referred to the imminence of doom. Jesus, in his mood of self-surrender, was fain to merge his identity with that of his few chosen disciples.

Was it really a fact that the good fellows in this narrow room, poor men, fishermen and peasants, lacking fire and faith, who had come with him from the Sea of Galilee to the Holy City, were now all his following? The great town was packed to bursting with the festival crowd; thousands upon thousands of hearts were swelling with solemn religious emotion : yet not one of them came hither, through that little door, to seek out the prophet, to make much of the man whose mission it was to achieve the conquest of Jerusalem ! That was why he was seized with a bodily yearning to enter into a veritable communion with the fellowship of his first and last disciples. Thus when, at the very end of the meal, he took another loaf and broke it in sunder, he felt as if it were his own outworn life which he was breaking up with his fingers. Offering the fragments to his companions with hands that were even more weary than when he had broken up the first loaf, he said in low tones :

" Take, eat : this is my body."

Then, in accordance with the custom, he prepared to dispatch the last cup of wine on its round. Watching the red sheen in the glass, he said (continuing the same train of thought) as he looked into the goblet :

" This is my blood of the new testament, which is shed for many. I will drink no more of the

fruit of the vine, until the day that I drink it
new in the kingdom of God."

He stood up, sang a hymn, and went out.   They
followed him, all but Judas, to the Mount of
Olives.

Judas stayed in the city.   It was his task to
summon the watch.

CHAPTER FIVE

PASSION

I.

UNDER a clear sky, it is cool when, late that
evening, Jesus and his companions slowly make
their way back to the Mount of Olives. The
noise of the town, keeping high festival, pursues
their footsteps, but the disciples heed it not, as
they move onward in silence, meditating upon
the words of the Master.

In him there is a change. Perhaps it is only
because the air strikes chill. It may be because
of Judas' disappearance, which he cannot fail
to have noticed. He may well have an increasingly urgent sense that danger presses. This
much is certain, that, after leaving the town,
he grows livelier; his aspect is brisk, and almost
combative. Maybe, at this last hour, he considers
the possibility of retreat, for he says to the
disciples :

"When I sent you without purse and scrip
and shoes, lacked ye anything ?"

"Nothing, Master."

"But now, he that hath a purse, let him take

it, and likewise his scrip ; and he that hath no sword, let him sell his garment, and buy one !"

They are startled, as if caught in the act. Some of them have indeed been letting their thoughts run upon the chances of armed resistance. Two among them, emboldened by this remarkable utterance, now venture to draw forth the weapons they have concealed about their persons, saying : " Lord, behold, here are two swords !" Whereupon he, shrinking back as of old when confronted with such actualities, recognises at sight of these poor iron tools how contradictory is the use of physical measures of defence when spirit and force, when God and the world, have to measure strength one against the other. He puts from him the fancy he has toyed with for a few fleeting seconds, and, with a double meaning, says quietly :

" It is enough."

Thoughts of the nearness of death are persistent. Sometimes he tries to mollify their bitterness by words from scripture. So now, he pauses in the ascent, and says (as if to put his disciples to the test) :

" All ye shall be offended because of me this night : for it is written, ' I will smite the shepherd, and the sheep of the flock shall be scattered abroad.' "

As at Cæsarea Philippi, Peter, in the ardour of his youthful zeal, is the readiest with a reply.

"Though all men shall be offended because of thee, yet will I never be offended!"

Jesus looks at Peter sadly. He knows the young man's eagerness, but feels that none of his disciples are to be depended upon—Peter no more than the rest. He shall be told as much in plain words :

"Verily I say unto thee that this night, before the cock crows, thou shalt deny me thrice!"

Peter rejoins : "Though I should die with thee, yet will I not deny thee." All the other disciples echo the words.

In Jesus, conflicting motives are at work. Is he really to surrender unresistingly to his enemies ? His disciples have just given him fresh assurances of loyalty. Some of them are armed. To-night he will not return to Bethany, the first place at which the authorities will look for him. If the vanished Judas be really in the plot, the traitor shall lead the foe thither in vain. Vestiges of combativeness flicker up in Jesus once more. Quitting the high-road, he bids the others follow him, and sets out in search of a place of refuge. On this last day of his life, Jesus looks for a hiding-place. He does so without plan, and too late, as he did all things that were done by him in conflict with what is usually called the real world. In the dead of night, they squeeze through the quickset hedge surrounding one of the olive orchards watered by the Brook Cedron on the western slope of the hill—a cactus hedge, doubtless, for these are burghers' fruit gardens, protected against thieves.

At length they are all within the enclosure. To the Master, a man of gentle disposition, such an intrusion into a fenced orchard is a new and disturbing experience, seeing that never before, in all his thirty-one years, has he thrust his way anywhere except into human hearts. Conspiratorial whispers, nocturnal searches for a lair, furtive crouchings and creepings, are no less unfamiliar. As a result of these strange happenings, the sense of joy in life, the animal spirits, with which he had bubbled over of yore, but which have been repressed during the winter wanderings, throughout the epoch of persecution, and still more during the recent days in the Holy City, reassert themselves in full force. Death, whose shape he has hitherto contemplated only through a mist of obscuring phraseology, now confronts him in hideous nakedness. The brooding stillness of the garden, the aromatic smell of the olives, the sheen of the stars, exercise their due effect on his emotions. The foretellings of scripture are forgotten, or seem ambiguous. As a natural result of these mingled influences, he is assailed with a burning desire for life. He will beseech the Father to let him live !

He is loath to unveil the confusion of his thoughts and feelings to the whole company of

his followers. Drawing apart, therefore, with the
three whom he loves best, and leaving the others
at rest beneath the trees, he goes on a little way
through the gloom. Trembling, afraid to be
alone, he says to Peter, James, and John :

"My soul is exceeding sorrowful unto death ;
tarry ye here, and watch !"

A few paces farther, and he throws himself
on the ground. With forehead and hair be-
dewed by the herbage, he prays :

"Father, all things are possible unto thee !
Take away this cup from me ! Nevertheless,
not what I will, but what thou wilt !"

He prays for life. Yet, as a dutiful son, even
while doing so he leaves the final decision to his
Father. Then, in agony of mind, he rises to
his feet once more. He has a sense of being
tracked down, like one who hears the voices of
pursuers ; he feels like a hunted beast when the
hounds are close at hand. Weak and helpless,
a poor mortal in sore distress, he turns back to
his dear companions for solace. Will not they
open their arms to receive him ? Will not his
friends help him in his affliction ?

He finds them sleeping. James, John, and
Peter are all asleep.

"Simon, sleepest thou ? Couldst thou not
watch one hour ?"

The disappointments of a lifetime are summed
up in these few words. The men who lie there

are the most devoted among his followers, the
ones to whom he has poured out his whole heart
for a year and more. Now, the first time their
friend and master craves aid from his fellow men,
and does not lean for support on God alone ;
when Jesus has been turning over in his mind
the enigma of his relation to God—this is the
moment when their senses are dulled by wine
and by the darkness. They lie there asleep !

Fresh doubts assail the prophet. Is it possible
that he has chosen the wrong path ? How often
has he seen this same Peter, wearied in body and
in mind, come to his wife for rest and refreshment, as a tired child runs to its mother. She,
for her part, opening her arms to him, would
help him as a mother helps a child. Had it
all been a mistake ? The refuge of women's
tender affection, gentle hands to stroke his hair,
soft lips to kiss his feet, loving-kindness to cherish
him in his daily doings—these would have been
his for the asking. He would have been able
to watch the growing-up of children, the little
children whom he loved. He would have spent
his life in the quiet Galilean township, one man
among many, and yet different from the rest,
for he would still have been privileged to hold
converse with the Father, on the hillside behind
the houses ; he could have kept his own counsel
about that matter !

Why did he go forth to carry the glad tidings

to his fellows, at the sacrifice of the quietude of
his own inner life ?   Where were those to whom
he could point as awakened and made happy
by his teaching ?   Simon, whom he had regarded
as the rock upon which the faith was to be
builded, and whom he had therefore called
Peter ; Simon was asleep in this hour of greatest
need. John, who had so often nestled into his
breast like a child, was asleep. James, too,
was asleep. Not one of them knew that their
friend was yearning for their help. They left
him to suffer anguish and terror alone. Perhaps
from first to last it had been an illusion ?   Perhaps
the strangers who had listened to his words, and the
sick whom he had cured, had long since forgotten
his message ?   Maybe those whose hearts he had
hoped to touch, drove the plough or sailed the
fishing-smack with the same dull indifference as
in the days before Jesus had crossed their path ?
If that and nothing more were the fruit of his
gospel, was such a mission worth dying for ?
" Father, all things are possible unto thee !
Take away this cup from me ! Nevertheless,
not what I will, but what thou wilt !"
    Now came a clamour, and the clash of weapons.
The hiding-place had been discovered. A band
of men carrying lanterns and torches pressed
into the garden.
    Their leader was the captain of the temple
guard.   Not being able, at this season of festival,

to withdraw many of his own company from the temple, he had started up a posse consisting mainly of the high priest's servitors, and had armed them with chance-found swords and staves and cudgels. They had been first to Bethany. Since Jesus was not there, they had returned towards the city, led by Judas, who scrutinised the roadside till he found traces of fugitives' passage. When the decisive moment came, he did not hesitate to carry out what he had determined; but he wished no injury to his brethren and friends, who had been fooled like himself. Since all the fugitives were hidden by the night ; since neither the captain nor his followers could be sure of recognising Jesus (whom they had seen on one occasion only, in a crowd) ; and since a man once arrested would not readily escape— Judas thought out a plan. He told the captain that he would give a sign. " Whomsoever I shall kiss, that same is he : hold him fast !"

Forthwith Judas goes up to Jesus, saying " Hail, Master," and kisses him. Thereupon, the captain's men hold up their lanterns, to make sure of their prey, and to see what he is like, while Jesus, looking his disciple in the face, says :

" Friend, wherefore art thou come ?"

The words have a paralysing effect upon the watch. On hearing Jesus call Judas " friend," even the high priest's servitors are amazed, draw

back, and ground their staves.   Every one of them
feels that there has been a betrayal.   Peter,
impetuous as usual, having a sword, draws it,
and, smiting at the nearest member of the posse,
hews off his right ear.   This is a signal for the
newcomers to lay hands, not upon the aggressor
(who has fled in the darkness), but on the man
who, too late, has tried to stay Peter's arm.

They lay hands on the Master.

At the instant when the torches first throw their
red light on the rugged faces of those who bear
them, when swords and helmets reflect the
gleam, when the power of the State confronts
him in the persons of its armed instruments, the
anguished and hunted man recovers his equa-
nimity ; he regains the poise which befits him
in face of world authority ; and the conviction
of being the Chosen One of God, reviving,
restores to him the pride which has been absent
during the last two days, and above all during
these night hours in the garden of Gethsemane.
Over and done with, at last, is the torment of
waiting.   The blow has fallen, and with certainty
has come a rebound.   In this solemn moment,
his first thought is to be faithful to his own
teaching.

" Put up again thy sword into its place, for all
they that take the sword shall perish by the
sword !"

Turning to the circle, and speaking rather to

his foes than to his friends, he raises his voice to deliver an essentially combative message :

" Think ye that I cannot now pray to my Father, and he shall give me more than twelve legions of angels ? But how then shall the scriptures be fulfilled ? . . . Are ye come out as against a thief with swords and staves for to take me ? I sat daily with you teaching in the temple, and ye laid no hold on me !"

The words beat on deaf ears. Not a soul understands him. The captain gives a sign, and his men lead Jesus away. The disciples are terrified, and make no attempt to rescue their master.

All of them betray him.

From among the olive trees comes the crackling of twigs and the rustling of garments, as they flee away in the darkness.

II.

An hour later, in the palace of the high priest, Jesus has been led through gateways and corridors, up broad staircases, and at length into a large room made airless and soundproof by thick hangings. By the light of the smoking tapers, he sees a semicircle of about twenty faces, the expectant faces of silent men, squatting on cushions. Then, from the middle of these, his gaze singles out one who has been sheltered and propped up by pillows and coverlets, a man of advanced age, with a fleshless and wrinkled countenance, yellow in colour and parchmenty in texture like the ancient rolls of the law he has seen in the temple. From this death-like mask proceed piping and gurgling sounds, which gradually form themselves into words.

This is Annas, who had been high priest a long while ago, in the happy times of Augustus. Five of his sons had been his successors in office. To-day, feared and hated, he still wields the power which the youngest of the five, Caiaphas (himself an old man by ordinary standards), now nominally holds as high priest chosen by the Roman overlords. For Caiaphas is the obedient son of his centenarian father. To-night, when the festival is in progress, it has been impossible to get together the whole of the Great Council. But, at short notice, a third of the members have assembled ; these will suffice. According to the law, a death sentence must be discussed one day, and confirmed the next. Since the matter is urgent, it will be enough to account this night-sitting as the first day, and morning (when it dawns) as the second.

For a death sentence is in view. The Sadducees who hold sway in the high-priestly house and in the Sanhedrim are not content, like the Pharisees, to discuss for ever, to talk without acting. One

who thinks that knows them little! They have
handed down the reins of power from one generation to another; and their wealth, too, passes
on by inheritance. They are monopolists, having
the exclusive right to sell doves and other victims,
for the sacrifice; they let out places to the dealers,
assign situations, fix prices.

If, in general, they are prone to look on indifferently, to remain inert, when the Pharisees
are already boiling over with wrath, they make
up for this by acting promptly and effectively
at critical moments, and thus nipping danger
in the bud. Such a moment has now come.
Witnesses are without. Here is the accused, still
unbound.

When the Galilean is brought before them,
these priests for whom priestcraft is in large
measure a political affair, men of ripe age and
wide experience, scrutinise him more closely
than he troubles to scrutinise them. They
compare his aspect and demeanour with those
of other lawbreakers; but he knows that his
case has been prejudged, and is content to maintain a formal appearance of interest. Although,
therefore, both parties are aware what the
upshot will be, the accusers who are sure of their
ground show more emotion than the doomed
man. Suppose that he were thunderingly to
denounce the intrigue against him, tear its
network to tatters, and thus appeal to the people?

What offences would the aged Annas find it
expedient to lay to his charge? The manner
of his entry into Jerusalem? The driving of
the money-changers from the temple? His invectives against the Pharisees?

Nothing of the sort happens. The witnesses,
a plurality of them as the Mosaic law directs,
testify to this, that, and the other. Old Annas,
it would seem, though he is accuser and judge
rolled into one, wants to give an impression of
impartiality. In the end, however, he loses
patience because the accused makes no answer
to any of the charges, and he himself directly
questions Jesus.

" What is thy doctrine? "

The prophet stands there amid his enemies.
Is he to disclose his innermost being to such as
these? He answers coldly :

" I spake openly to the world ; I ever taught
in the synagogues and in the temple, whither
the Jews always resort ; and I have hidden
nothing. Why askest thou me? Ask those who
heard me, what I said unto them. Behold, they
know what I said."

Never yet had any one dared to speak thus to
the aged questioner. Even before Annas had
time to admonish the offender, one of the
servitors of the temple struck Jesus with the
palm of his hand, saying : " Answerest thou the
high priest so? "

Jesus rejoined quietly, phrasing his reply after
the manner of the Pharisees : " If I have spoken
evil, bear witness of the evil ; but if well, why
smitest thou me ?"

The priests disapprove of this rough handling
of the accused. All should be done decently
and in order. But old Annas, recognising that
he will get no further on his present line, calls
witnesses who can testify to the gravest of Jesus'
crimes. They join in declaring that they recently
heard him say : " I will destroy this temple that
is made with hands, and within three days I will
build another made without hands."

Again the accused is silent. No doubt he did
say something of the kind, for the habitations in
the kingdom of God, the abiding places of genuine
piety, do not need years for their building—or
else they need an eternity. Now Annas leans
forward from among his cushions, pushes aside
one of the coverlets, and enquires ; " Answerest
thou nothing ?"

No sound breaks the stillness in the thickly
curtained room. The assessors look at one
another wonderingly. Why does not their venerable chief proceed to count the votes. The
accused does not deny the blasphemy with which
he has been charged. But the shrewd old man
who presides has been taught by long experience.
He wants firmer ground, for he knows the " yea
and nay " of the Pharisees, their fondness for

raising objections when a decision has become
irrevocable ; and he knows the curt and gruff
ways of the Roman governor, who always insists
upon having indisputable warrant before taking
action. A frank admission must therefore be
extorted from the false prophet, and Annas at
length touches upon the most dangerous question
of all, uses a word of power which must surely
tempt Jesus to lay aside the mask of impassivity.
Stretching out his silk-clad arms, as if he would
touch the threadbare robe of the accused, he
says : " Tell us : art thou the Messiah ?"

Once again there is a conflict within Jesus
between his faith in his own mission and his
contempt for those who question it ; dignity is at
war with loathing ; pride is arrayed against
pride. Once again he evades the issue, and is
content to say :

" If I tell you, ye will not believe. But if I
should ask you, ye will not answer me, nor let
me go !"

The assessors become ever more wrathful at
the frowardness of the accused, and at what seems
to them the undue forbearance of their chief.
But Annas sticks to his point. With an old man's
obstinacy and a priest's cunning, he moves on
towards his goal. He set out to force an avowal
from Jesus, and now he summons all his energies
for this purpose. He wants to rise to his feet,
and as soon as he rests his tremulous arms upon

the cushion on which he sits, his sons who are
on either side of him make haste to help him,
knowing that nowadays he only makes a move
to stand up when he wishes to call upon God's
holy name. Slowly the wizened form—little
more than a skeleton decked out in silk—rises
from among the coverlets and cushions. The
ancient lifts his bony hand, and croakingly
apostrophises the accused :

"I adjure thee by the living God that thou
tell us whether thou be the Christ, the Son of
God !"

Now Jesus feels that the moment has come
when he must, in the heart of his enemies' camp,
make the open avowal so solemnly demanded of
him. Yet it is in the tone of humility which
characterised him in the earlier days of his mission
that he answers, softly :

"Thou hast said it."

An instant later he raises an arm, glances round
the half-circle of his judges, and, in his other
voice, the voice proper to his regal dignity, he
exclaims :

"Nevertheless I say unto you, hereafter ye
shall see the Son of Man sitting on the right
hand of power, and coming in the clouds of
heaven !"

All spring to their feet. Tension is succeeded
by alarm, as if they had expected a different
answer. That which for an hour they have been

eagerly awaiting, comes in the end (when boldly
uttered) as a blow. Daniel's words, that the
Messiah would sit by God's throne—he has
twisted them to his own uses ! With trembling
hands old Annas plucks at his garments, striving
to rend them. His thin voice is more hopelessly
cracked than ever, as he overstrains it in the
attempt to shout denunciation : " He hath
spoken blasphemy ! What further need have we
of witnesses ? Behold, now ye have heard his
blasphemy ! What think ye ?"

" He is guilty unto death !" comes the answer
from them all.

There is a general feeling of relief. This
nocturnal arrest, this secret trial—there had
undoubtably been a flavour of partisanship about
them. But now the prophet is self-condemned
by the terms of the prevailing law. He has
attempted high treason against the theocracy,
and must pay the penalty of failure. Many have
been guilty of high treason, many prophets,
before and after the Nazarene, have been
sentenced and executed in due form of law—
only, like Jesus, to be commemorated in later
days with statues and extolled in song.

The dignity of a court of justice, a dignity
whose semblance has hitherto been upheld, is
scattered to the winds. Fasting and lamentation,
prescribed by the law before every execution, are
forgotten. They crowd round the condemned

man, deride him and buffet him, as if to assure
themselves of his weakness ; then they thrust him
contumeliously forth from the room, to wait
outside till they can bring him to Pilate's hall
of judgment when day dawns.

Meanwhile, of all the disciples, Peter alone
had repented of his cowardly flight. Towards
morning, an impulse of shame drove him to
follow his master, and he slipped furtively into
the high priest's palace. There, in the anteroom,
the servants were seated round the fire, discussing
the events of the night. Peter drew near and
sought to glean information. Among the men-
servants was a maid laughing and jesting with
them. This damsel had seen the prophet and
his followers in the temple. Now, catching sight
of Peter, she recognised him, and exclaimed:
" Thou also wast with Jesus of Nazareth."

Peter was prompt to deny, saying : " I know
him not, neither understand I what thou
sayest."

Others have marked his coming, and after
a little while one of these draws the stranger
forward into the firelight, the better to scan his
face, and then says : " Did I not see thee with
him overnight in the garden ?"

" It was not I," rejoins Peter.

Then a third, who notes the rustic accent,
says at a venture, but confidently : " Of a truth
this fellow also was with him, for he is a

Galilean." And to Peter: "Thy speech bewrayeth thee!"

Peter, still sedulous to deny, begins to curse and swear, and reiterate : " I know not the man !"

Withdrawing unobtrusively from the circle by the fire, he slinks away to the gate. There, through the bars, he hears the crowing of the cock in the outer court, is reminded of the Master's prophecy, goes forth, and weeps bitterly.

Shortly after daybreak, the condemned man is brought before the assembled Sanhedrim. The evidences of the witnesses and the prisoner's own avowal are briefly recapitulated. Without more ado, the Great Council confirms the decision of the Small. Thereupon all rise and prepare to go to the governor, for no death sentence is valid without his sanction, and upon him devolves the carrying of it into effect. In solemn procession, the seventy councillors make their way to the fortress of Antonia, the condemned man, bound, in their midst.

III.

Only during the festival did Pilate reside in the fortress. At this time all its gates and bridges were guarded by the Roman cohorts with especial care. It became the police headquarters. Thousands of strangers in the city looked, some

with fear and some with veneration, westward
across the gorge, to the place where the imperial
stronghold towered above the buildings in the
upper town. A huge crowd flocked in the wake
of the priests, when these were seen to be mount-
ing towards the fortress, robed in festal array.
But the Jews could not enter the heathen castle,
for they would be defiled by doing so at the
season of Passover. Long ere this, therefore,
the difficulty had been met by the erection of a
wooden courthouse just outside the fortifications,
so that the Roman governor could continue to
act as supreme judge during the period of his
residence at Antonia.

When the procession drew near, Pilate, who
had doubtless been forewarned, came forth from
the gate, surrounded by his officers and lictors.
He stood to receive Caiaphas, the high priest,
spokesman of the Great Council. Looking at the
bound figure in the midst of the priests, the
Roman said curtly : " What accusation bring
ye against this man ?" When governor and high
priest met unwatched in the former's private
apartments, both were wont to be extremely
courteous in their demeanour, and sought the
best way to a mutual understanding ; for Rome
wanted willing subjects, and Caiaphas wanted a
friendly ruler. But to-day, under the public
eye, Pilate has to represent the grandeur of Rome,
and is therefore cold, blunt, and forbidding.

His chief desire is, as always, to avoid espousing
the cause of any particular faction of the Jews.
It may be for this reason, or it may be because
he is impressed by the aspect of a prisoner whose
doings have long been known to him by repute,
that he now gives a sign to the lictors, who
separate Jesus from the priests and take him
through the gateway into the judgment hall
within the castle. Then he turns back to the
priests, who shout accusations : " We found this
fellow perverting the nation, and forbidding to
give tribute to Cæsar "—until Caiaphas imposes
silence on them, and says to Pilate :

" The man calls himself Christ, the King of the
Jews !"

The high priest was acting on his father's
instructions, for the crafty Annas wished the
whole affair to be given a new complexion.
The religious question, which did not interest
their pagan rulers, was to be thrust unto the
background ; and its place to be taken by a
political one. What had been the trial of a
schismatic, was to become the trial of a traitor
against Rome. Pilate, however, was at a loss,
and went back through the gate to interrogate
the accused.

Jesus, meanwhile had been standing in the
hall of judgment, looking tranquilly at what was
there to see. This inner hall was a fine stone
structure, richly ornamented. Beyond it was a

pleasure garden, with attractive paths, and a turreted open reservoir, over and round which doves were wheeling.

"So this is how the great ones of the world live," says Jesus to himself. Never before has he been in a palace or a castle. Now that he sees its luxury, he feels no rancour. The stillness does him good.

Pilate comes in, and questions him in the abrupt way usual in enquiries of the sort. Probably he speaks Greek, and the accused finds it difficult to understand.

"Art thou the King of the Jews?"

A congenial sense of warmth floods the prophet's veins. How often has he felt like this when in the company of the heathen, who are not so apt to be afflicted with self-righteousness as are the Jews! Perhaps he had an inkling that the soldiers in whose hands his fate lies may share with him sentiments that are certainly lacking in the priests outside there, for he answers Pilate's question with another:

"Sayest thou this of thyself, or did others tell it thee of me?"

With a twinkle in his eye, the governor rejoins, quite in the style of a Jewish disputation: "Am I a Jew?" Then, resuming his official manner, he goes on: "Thine own nation and the chief priests have delivered thee unto me. What hast thou done?"

Again Jesus is impelled to explain to the pagan a thing which his fellow countrymen who are his enemies have never understood. Perhaps now, when his career is drawing to a close, he will find in this soldier one able to understand the handicraftsman. In the tone of the old Nazareth days, with the gentle, melting voice of that vanished time, he says (and it sounds like a sublime avowal) :

" My kingdom is not of this world. If my kingdom were of this world, then would my servants fight, that I should not be delivered to the Jews."

The governor listens to him with astonishment. The man is apparently an enthusiast. Maybe a use might be made of him ! The Jews are often refractory, and Jesus might help to keep them in order. Pilate therefore asks, with lively interest :

" Art thou, then, a king ?"

Jesus nods assent. He sees the pagan's drift, and rejoins :

" Yes, I am a king. To this end was I born, and for this cause came I into the world, that I should bear witness unto the truth. Everyone that is of the truth, heareth my voice."

Never before had he described his mission in such mundane terms. But Pilate thinks : " Merely a philosopher after all. Nothing to be done with him in that case !" Somewhat

disdainfully (and yet not wholly in contempt),
Pilate rejoins :

" What is truth ?"

For a moment they stand face to face, the
Jewish prisoner and the Roman governor, in
the judgment hall of the fortress, surrounded by
swords and helmets.   One of them is armed, and
clad in a short toga ; the other is weaponless, and
wears a long gray mantle.   They confront one
another exchanging thoughts ; as though they
were not accused and judge, beggar and lord, as
though one of them were not fighting for the life
which the other weighs in his mailed hand ;
rather as though the beggar were a king, and the
governor an emperor's envoy, but nothing more
than the poor servant of his duty.   Thus do Jesus
and Pilate confront one another, reflective,
waiting on one another's words, questioning—
until one of them speaks of " truth," and thereby
the man of the world and the prophet are torn
asunder.

Going back to the Jews outside, Pilate, fully
composed once more, says to them : " I find no
fault in this man."

There is a chorus of expostulation : " He
stirreth up the people, teaching throughout all
Jewry, like Judas the rebel, who likewise began
in Galilee !"

Galilee ? Amid the clamour, this word gives
a clear lead to the Roman. The period of

communion upon abstract topics is over. Once
more he is dominated by the wish to find a course
that will most effectively gratify the numerous
and conflicting demands that are voiced in this
amazing theocracy. As soon as he hears that
Jesus is a Galilean, he sees a way of escape from
his perplexities. Galilee does not belong to
Rome, but to Herod ; and Herod is in Jerusalem
—had visited him no longer ago than yesterday.
Without vouchsafing a word in answer to the
clamour, the governor goes back into the fortress,
and, by a postern gate, sends the prisoner in
charge of a centurion and a few soldiers to Herod,
with an enquiry whether the tetrarch would not
like to take over the case, since the Galilean
comes within his jurisdiction.

During the last few days, Herod had been much
disquieted by rumours to the effect that John had
risen from the dead, and had come to Jerusalem.
Doubtless he had kept himself informed as to the
doings of Jesus and of those who sought to lay
Jesus low ; and he must have heard of the trial
and the death sentence that morning. Now,
when the prophet was brought in, Herod looked
at him with mingled curiosity and uneasiness.
No, Jesus was not in the least like John ! Still,
this Galilean seer might well be able to utter
some wise saying ; might be able with a single
phrase to dispel the feelings of horror with which
the tetrarch was afflicted whenever thoughts of

the murdered Baptist invaded his mind. Herod, therefore, " questioned him in many words "— whose purport has not come down to us.

Jesus would give no answer. When brought before Herod, his only thought was : " This is the man but for whom my whole career would have been different, but for whom I should, perhaps, never have adopted a public career at all ; but for whom, certainly, my life would never have come to this pass, would not have been drawing to a close to-day." Was he to answer such a man's questions, read the stars, foretell the future ? He was silent, though a few care-fully chosen words might have saved his life ; was silent, because he no longer thought of being rescued by human hands ; was silent, because both the Jewish tetrarch and the pagan governor were but phantoms before the eyes of one whose vision could pierce the clouds of heaven.

Herod, therefore, came to the conclusion that he was no more than a fool, one who had assumed John's mantle without inheriting any of that prophet's sardonic wisdom. He was an object for mockery. The tetrarch had him arrayed in a white robe, and sent him back to Pilate as a witless imbecile.

Pilate's wife, meanwhile, seated at the window of her room, had been looking down at the prophet of whom during these days she had heard many tales of wonder. During the years spent among

the Jews, she had pondered deeply concerning
the things she had heard both from philosophers
in Rome and Alexandria, and from Hebrew
teachers here in Palestine. Superstition was at
work in her as well as knowledge ; and the
sympathy aroused in all women who set eyes on
the Nazarene, doubtless played its part. She
sent a warning message to her husband : " Have
thou nothing to do with that just man. Last
night I suffered many things in a dream because
of him !"

Her admonition helps to reinforce the Roman's
first impression that Jesus is nothing more than
a harmless enthusiast. He is annoyed by the
importunacy of these self-seeking priests, who
wish, for the advantage of school or sect, to
sacrifice one who may be their rival in popular
favour. Going out to the assembled Jews for
the third time, he says : " Ye have brought this
man unto me as one that perverteth the people.
I, having examined him, have found no fault
in him. No, nor yet Herod. I will therefore
chastise him and let him go." Thus the issue
hangs in the wind, as the Jews and the governor
face one another.

At this juncture, there arrives on the scene a
rabble of persons who have come to celebrate a
popular custom. Year by year at the Passover the
Romans grant amnesty to one condemned Jewish
criminal, whose liberation is regarded as symbolic

of the deliverance of the Israelites out of Egypt—
with the added implication that thereby the
strictness of Roman rule and the indignity of
Hebrew servitude are mitigated. Having run
through the streets, they reach the gate of the
fortress, and clamour there like children, rather
for the granting of an established right than
because they have any wish to save a life :

" It is Passover !   Deliver up to us a prisoner !"

Surely this must be a sign ?   Pilate says to the
leader : " Will ye that I release unto you the
King of the Jews ?"

The mob does not notice the undertone of
contempt with which the words are spoken.   The
priests, too, have something else to think of than
fine shades of meaning.   They know the fickle
humour of their own people.   A phrase, an
exclamation, multiplied a thousandfold by the
many-throated crowd, and the dangerous
prophet (whom Rome seems inclined to protect)
will be set at liberty.   One of their number hits
upon an idea.   There is another prisoner, Barabbas by name, the most recent of the champions
of Jewish freedom, who are thorns in the side of
the priesthood, but ever the darlings of the mob.
A disciple of Judas the insurgent, a zealot like his
great forerunner, he had last autumn invaded the
capital at the head of a handful of Galileans, and
had been arrested after he and his followers had
insulted and molested the Roman watch.   As

a catchword, this priest throws out the name of
Barabbas.

" Barabbas !" The members of the Great
Council, grasping the significance of the utterance, were quick to echo it. Those who stood
nearest, took up the cry. In a moment every
one was shouting " Barabbas," including many
who now heard of him for the first time.

" Not this man, but Barabbas ! Away with
this man, and release unto us Barabbas !"

Even yet, Pilate would fain save Jesus from the
priests, but if he is to decide the case against
them he needs the support of the people. The
festal season will justify a second act of clemency,
and he disclosed this possibility by asking those
to whom he leaves the decision :

" What will ye then that I shall do unto him
whom ye call the King of the Jews ?"

" Crucify him !" shout the priests with one
voice. " Crucify him !" comes in chorus from
the crowd—though many of those that join in
the demand do not even know for whose cruci-
fixion they clamour. Such is still the universal
cry of the mob, when two thousand years have
come and gone.

The Roman makes one more effort, tests the
temper of the rabble yet again, asking :

" Why ? What evil hath he done ?"

One of the shrewdest among his hearers has an
answer ready :

" Whosoever maketh himself a king, speaketh against Cæsar. If thou let this man go, thou art not Cæsar's friend !"

Pilate smiles inwardly. With a prompt change of front, he endeavours to secure a yet more open expression of this remarkable display of friendship for Rome on the part of the Jewish people. It will be something he can report, with an excellent effect on his own prospects. To spur on the multitude in the direction he wants them to pursue, he enquires :

" Shall I crucify your king ?"

" We have no king but Cæsar !"

Thereupon the governor gives a sign to the legionaries at the gate, that they may bring out the prisoner.

He, meanwhile, has been transformed.

What time Pilate has been parleying without, the soldiers within have been amusing themselves. The governor had said that the man was to be scourged in any case, so they had stripped him of the white robe put on by Herod's orders, and had beaten him with rods. Then, when he was about to clothe himself again, the fancy had taken them to dress him up as the King he was fabled to be. One of them threw a military cloak round his shoulders, and fastened the clasp ; another put a reed sceptre in his hand ; a third, cutting some thorns from the garden hedge, plaited them into a crown to surmount the victim's long hair.

When, in this guise, Jesus comes out through the gate, still silent; when the crowd utters shouts of ribald laughter ; when all is lost—then Pilate, the man of the world, is once again aware of a feeling of respect for the strange enthusiast. Pointing to the crowned figure, he says to the centurions standing close at hand (speaking Latin, so that no one else shall understand the words) :

" Ecce homo !"

IV.

How heavy the cross is, and the way seems long. Death will be easy enough. Indeed, it will not be death at all, for the Father will hold out loving arms, and the glories of heaven will be opened !

The day is hot, and this cedar wood is heavy. The crosspiece and the upright are hollowed out, so as to dovetail into one another. Roughly done, but strong enough to bear a man's weight.

No cross is needed to carry him into the kingdom of heaven, through the blue sky ; nothing but the Father's grace. When will it be vouchsafed ? Will his face be hidden in the clouds, or plainly visible ? Will he wrap the

cross in mist, and lift it up with its living burden ?
The prophets used to say that to see God was to
die. Perhaps, therefore, he will not show himself, will only send his dove, as he did beside
Jordan, when his voice sounded like far-off
thunder. Never since then had he spoken so
clearly and softly. " My beloved son." Those
words had never been repeated, though Peter
said he had heard them on the mountain near
Cæsarea Philippi. They would be heard again
to-day.

Why do the soldiers of the escort drive him
forward so ruthlessly ? Do they wish him ill ?
Oh, no, they are only carrying out their orders,
and the centurion who commands them is
merely carrying out the will of the priests. If
the priests fail to recognise God, is it their fault ?
They do not know whom they are killing. They
do not know what they are doing. Perhaps God
is nearer to them than they are aware. True,
they seemed wrathful and hostile, but the mob
urged them on. As for Pilate, he acted at their
instigation. " An hour's talk with that Roman,
and he would have followed me ! Whither ?
Back to the Sea of Galilee ! Fruit does not ripen
here. Jerusalem is a place of stone."

The cross is too heavy for him ; the sap is
still in the wood. That young fellow passing by
is vigorous. Let him carry it for the condemned
man—not very far, now. A kindly-looking fellow,

he carries another's cross, and has received the new message in his heart though he has never heard it with his ears. Thus in the last hour there comes a new disciple. But where are the others?

While the cross is thus borne forwards on a young man's powerful shoulders, there totters along behind it the pale figure of the prophet, suddenly grown old, pushed and jostled by the soldiers of the escort.

The centurion in command rides beside the train in gloomy silence. The officer and his men are out of humour, for they regard such executioner's work as beneath a soldier's dignity, and they loathe the tedium of waiting. Last time they had had to spend two days under the cross before the victim died.

Up there on the hill, more legionaries are already at work hammering and delving, for there are two other crucifixions to-day. Jews expiating the crimes of theft and murder. While some of the soldiers are digging holes in the ground, others are nailing the criminals to the crosses as these lie flat upon the soil. One of them resists; but strong hands hold him fast, his yells are ignored, and the huge nails are driven home, one through each hand, and one through both feet. Nail them firmly, so that no cord need be wasted on the malefactors! Now, up with the cross! The feet are supported by the

projecting board to which they are nailed, and
the fork of the legs by a little seat slanting back-
wards, which prevents the body from falling
forwards, and, with its weight, rending the hands
from the nails. A number of soldiers working
together, they lower the base of the cross into
the hole which has been prepared, and shovel
in earth and stones to make it stand firmly.
Thus almost simultaneously the two crosses with
the thieves nailed to them are set up in the
scorching sunlight, and the air is rent with the
screams of the tortured men.

He whose turn is now to come sees all this as
if in a dream. "Murderers and thieves," he
thinks ; " poor men, led astray, sentenced, and
hurried off to their doom !" Above the head of
each a placard has been affixed, declaring in
three languages the nature of the offenders'
crimes. There must be such a placard for him,
too. Yes, that thickset little soldier, the one who
had kicked him just now, is nailing it to his cross.
" Rex Judæorum." Had he ever used that
name of himself? Perhaps the whole thing is
the illusion of men whom God has struck with
blindness ? Soon the Father will manifest himself in glory and in truth !

While he thus continues to indulge in hopeful
fantasies, he suddenly becomes aware that his
arms have been seized by pitiless hands, and that
he has been stretched on the cross. He watches

a nail, which looms gigantic before his eyes.
Horror overwhelms him ; pain racks him ; he
faints.

When he comes to his senses again, and grows
aware of the fiery smart in his wounds, he turns
his head to right and to left, and the sight of the
other crosses recalls him to an understanding of
what has happened. Certainly he has not
awakened in heaven ! On the ground, the
soldiers have settled down for their long vigil.
Some are drinking, others dicing. He recognises
his own vesture, for which they are casting lots.
Now, when he groans, one of them looks up,
another gives a sign, a sponge tied to a stick
is lifted to his lips, and a soldier, speaking in
Greek, tells him to drink, for it will dull his pain.

Not until then does he fully realise the situation.
Summoning up his last reserves of energy, he
shakes his aching head in refusal. The man
below shrugs his shoulders, and the sponge is
withdrawn. Jesus does not wish to benumb
himself. Is he to miss the moment for which
he has so long been waiting, simply in order to
ease the pain in his hands ? If only the disciples
were here, to see God's grace, about to be
manifested !

But the disciples are far away, and there are
very few spectators, for every one is celebrating
the Passover in that harsh city couched upon its
hills of stone. Jerusalem ! Something shines

brightly in the distance to the left. That is
the temple. There he had hoped to gain a
victory. What had he achieved? Had he not
made a deadly onslaught upon the priests?
No doubt they had felt that he was the herald
of a new order, before whose words the old
temple would crumble. What a tremendous
struggle! When would it end?

Two passers-by look up at him from the road.
One of them calls out scornfully: " Ah, thou that
destroyest the temple, and buildest it again in
three days!" Jesus hears the taunt. Mastering
his agony, to listen further, he hears the other
say: " Let Christ the King of Israel descend
now from the cross, that we may see and
believe!"

He trembles. Are these wayfarers right after
all? When will the saving miracle be wrought?
Now from the cross on the right comes another
voice, rancorous with hate. One of his crucified
companions has also heard the gibe, and repeats
it, shouting: " Yes, if thou be Christ, save
thyself and us."

But, from his left, the other despairing wretch
cries in reproof: " Art thou not ashamed?
We are justly condemned, and receive due
reward of our deeds, being malefactors! This
man has done nothing amiss!" Then, to Jesus,
he says: " Lord, remember me when thou
comest into thy kingdom."

To Jesus, the words are like a ray of light. No
matter that the Roman soldiers laugh to hear
these crucified Jews wrangling. What Jesus
hears is the voice of one who believes in him.
This thief and murderer feels the power of the
Son of Man, whose sinking hopes revive. Through
the mouth of one of the lowliest of his brethren,
God is exhorting him to be steadfast in the faith.
Once more there has been a word about his
kingdom, a word from on high, out of the firmament, though only spoken on a cross. He
answers (so softly that the other can scarcely hear
him) :

" This very night thou shall be with me in
paradise."

This very night ! He still hopes, then ! Soon,
very soon, the Father will deliver him. It
cannot really be his Father's wish that he should
suffer these cruel pains in body and limbs. He
has wrestled for faith ever since the dove and the
voice of God came to tell him that he was to
forsake his handicraft and to proclaim the kingdom of the Father. Was this faith a deception ?
Was the vision an illusion ? Why, then, should
he have been put to such a test ? Why should
he have been seized and nailed to a cross, iron
nails driven through hands that had never
struck a blow ? If all this were but transitory
suffering, why should it be so agonising, and why
should it last so long ?

Pangs of body and tortures of mind become interwoven one with another, simultaneously confusing him and enlightening him. His thoughts are like arrows, fiery arrows, resembling the shafts of the noonday sun, descending mercilessly out of the blue upon burning forehead and scorched limbs. His eyes rove in search of disciples and friends.

All have fled.

There is not one to give the Master a last consolation, and, in his sorest need, to strengthen him with his own teachings. Not one to hear the prophet's last words, and hand them down to posterity.

Just as overnight they had fallen asleep at Gethsemane, and had taken to flight when his enemies had seized him, so now, it would seem, their zeal had fallen asleep. His influence was at an end ; their faith had vanished ; his message had fallen on deaf ears ; the springs of brotherly love had dried up. All had been in vain ! The only onlookers were two or three women, thickly veiled, standing a long way off. They seemed to be weeping. Were they afraid to call a greeting ? His mother was far away ; so were his brothers and his sisters. Those who stand there and sob are not his kinswomen. They are the strangers who have followed him in his wanderings. The one among them who is suffering most keenly is one that had been a sinner, the woman who, in the little town beside the Sea of Galilee, had aforetime dried his feet with her hair. These women of the people, wives and daughters of poor fishermen, are the last persons on whom he sets eyes. They, at least, have understood the message of love. But where are the thousands? Will any vestige remain of his teaching last summer? If the disciples scatter, who will record his message? If that message passes without leaving a trace, must he not have been rating himself too high? Perhaps, after all, he was just such a man as his own brothers, who deemed him possessed!

As the slow minutes ebb away, pain chases pain through his tortured frame, as if it were being seared with fire, devoured by beasts of prey.

At length, when ages, as it seems, have passed; when he feels that the heart in his frail body is breaking; when intelligence and imagination are clouded, and faith and hope are obscured; when all his consciousness is filled with pain—he breaks the silence he has kept throughout these dreadful hours. The torment of mind and body finds vent in a heart-rending cry. The doubts which had assailed him yester-eve in the garden have been multiplied a thousandfold in his dolorous situation on the cross. The craving to escape from this sacrificial death takes the form of a complaint. In these seconds of the final agony, dreams of a life transcending that of mortals no longer sustain him. The Father, to whom he has given himself with such devout faith, has turned away from the most loving of sons. No longer does God look down from his palace above the clouds into this world of suffering men. His spirit is remote from earth, and his heart beats only in heaven. The world is a lost world; the Son is alone; the Father is no Father. Lonely and helpless, a human body is parching, and a human heart is breaking. Jesus cries :

" My God, my God, why hast thou forsaken me ?"

The soldiers, hearing this cry, stop their dicing. Glancing up, the centurion orders one of his men to moisten from a flask the sponge on which the benumbing drink had before been offered to the crucified. It is lifted to the dying man's lips. He opens them, and sucks in the moisture. The pain returns in full force to his tortured limbs, and he utters a loud cry.

This cry of agony and despair ends a life which for thirty years has expressed itself in the gentle tones of love that brings solace to others, in the voiceless song of an affectionate human heart.

V.

" Dead so soon ?" enquires Pilate, when a
member of the Great Council comes to him and
asks for the body of Jesus. According to Roman
custom, the corpse of an executed criminal
belongs to the relatives or friends, and this dis-
tinguished man has now avowed his faith in the
prophet. Not until the centurion, having been
summoned, confirms the statement that the
Galilean has died after no more than a few hours
on the cross, does the governor consent that his
body shall be taken down without having the
legs broken—for the legs of the other two victims
are broken to speed their death, since the Sabbath
is at hand, and all must be over before then.

Hastily, that no one else shall meddle in the
matter, the stranger and the women lift him
from the cross. Wrapping the body in a white
shroud, they carry it to a newly made tomb in
the councillor's garden, a tomb which he has
had hewn out of the rock for himself. After the
Sabbath, they will arrange for an interment in
due form. All they want to-day is to make sure
of a provisional burial, without interference on
the part of the priests. That is why they are so
speedy, as if upon a flight. No incense ; no
anointing. Enough to roll a great stone to the
door of the sepulchre, for the evening star is

already shining, and no more work must be done till the Sabbath is over.

Next evening, the women come back, bringing spices and unguents, to prepare the body for burial. Mary Magdalen will anoint the corpse, as before she had anointed the feet of the living man. Who will roll away the stone for them ? They are not strong enough, and there is no man to be seen. But when they reach the sepulchre, they find that the stone has already been rolled away, and that the body has vanished !

Next day, all Jerusalem has heard the news. A hundred rumours chase one another through the city. Some say that Pilate has regretted giving Jesus' body to his friends, and has had it hidden. A second story is that the priests have stolen the corpse, lest the multitude should idolise it. A third notion is that the gardener must be at the bottom of what has happened, being afraid that a great concourse at the tomb would trample his flowers. According to a fourth version, some of the rascals who plunder tombs of anything they can get money for must have been at work. A fifth theory is that of those who say that no one has ever died after only three hours on the cross; that the Nazarene's disciples have revived Jesus from apparent death, and have got him away into safe hiding. The priests go to Pilate, berate him for being so pliable, and foretell a peck of troubles, now that the prophet's followers have been allowed to steal the body, in order to tell the people that their Master has risen from the dead.

But the women, who love him, believe that in waking dreams they have seen the risen Jesus in the flesh.

Billing & Sons, Limited,
PRINTERS,
Guildford and Esher.